XFactor for Generation Y

10 Key Steps for Personal & Career Development

Stuart K. P. Howard

Authority
PRESS

Published by Authority Press, Inc.
2360 Corporate Circle
Suite 400
Henderson, NV 89074
Authority-Press.com

Manufactured in the United States of America.

ISBN: 978-1-62865-059-4

Contents

Foreword

If you are Generation 'Y', seeking your first job, starting a new role, looking to move to your first management position or just wanting to improve yourself, then this book is a must-read for you.

In this powerful and easy-to-read book you will find the X-Factors required to take you one step ahead of the crowd and give you a competitive edge in your job search or career.

This is your 'one-on-one' coach in a book. Keep this book with you and refer to it often and you will find the X-Factors you need at the time you need them.

The book covers key areas such as developing your emotional intelligence, knowing your strengths, goal setting, leadership style and how to drive change in your organization.

Raymond Aaron
New York Times Best Selling Author
www.MillionaireBusinessBootcamp.com

Acknowledgements

To Anne, my wife, life-long friend and supporter of all that I do.

My son, Philip, Generation Y, for his initial inspiration to write this book and constructive input

My daughter, Joanna, Generation Y, for writing assistance & marketing

David Currie, the valleys are not so deep & mountaintops are much higher with a true friend by my side

Rosanna Altman, Generation Y, for editorial critique of the work & cover design

Goodyear Dunlop Tires for their management and personal development training programs

Nir Pearlshtein for illustrations

Chapter 1

Discover your Strengths

"If you spend your life trying to be good at everything, you will never be great at anything."
— Tom Rath

Introduction

Understanding yourself is the key to realizing your hopes and dreams. It is the key to understanding your mindset and what drives you to succeed. Only when you discover yourself can you learn to manage yourself, set and achieve goals and in turn be all that you can be. You can then achieve what Abraham Maslow describes as 'Self Actualization.' It is a long way to the top of Maslow's pyramid! After your *physiological* needs are met then you require *safety* and a sense of *belonging* to a family, community, team or organization. Then comes *self -esteem* and *self -confidence*. You can only gain real confidence in yourselves when you start to know yourselves and therefore you need a process to help you in this self discovery.

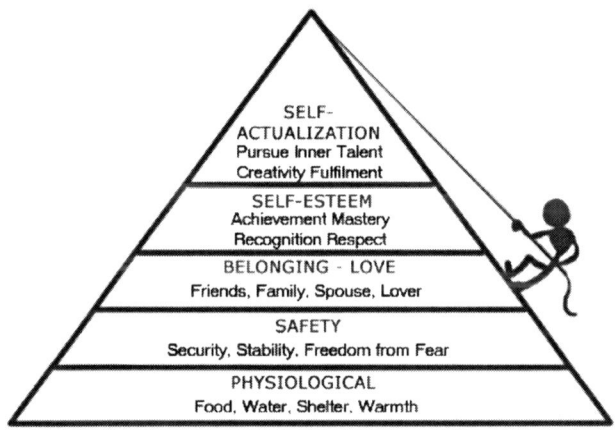

Abraham Maslow's Pyramid of Needs

Self Discovery

John Wooden, American Basketball coach, said, "Five years from now, you're the same person except for the people you've met and the books you've read." I want to tell you of one such person and one such book. In 2008, while in the office of Silvia Sitzen, Human Resources Director for Goodyear Tires, we were discussing personal development. Silvia made the comment that a sports coach would never ask a marathon runner to run 100m and never ask a sprinter to attempt a marathon. The message was clear, if you focus on the weak areas of your life, the skills that you are not so good at or the things you don't have a natural bias for, then you will not succeed to be all that you can be. You will end up like the marathon runner trying to run the 100m; you will lose, you will become despondent, discouraged and start to lose confidence. You will neither be a good marathon runner nor a good sprinter and be mediocre at best and never fulfill your goals. Silvia gave me the important lesson that we should all work to our strengths. She gave me a copy of *Strengths Finders* by Markus Buckingham. [1] This encounter was a pivotal point in my lifelong learning and personal development. John Wooden was correct; I was a different person after my meeting with Silvia and after reading the book, she gave me.

The Mirror

The *Strengths Finders* book describes 34 key 'strengths' or 'themes.' These are the main character traits that we all have. While reading the book you start to relate to a few of the key themes and start to understand yourself a little more. The book acts like a mirror and slowly reveals to you the key strengths that you have.

A mirror [2] shows areas where you are strong and areas where you are not so strong. Reflect on what you enjoy doing, what do you not enjoy? Why do you do that task or job? Why do you pursue that job, career or hobby? Do you like to engage with people, procedures or technology? Ask a friend, work colleague or partner to assist you to reflect on these questions. Identify your strengths and when you are ready write your top 5 key strengths below. In the words of Napoleon Hill, "Take inventory of mental assets and liabilities, you will discover that your greatest weakness is lack of self-confidence." [3] Focus only on your strengths, where you excel.

It may be the first time you have considered these questions; however, take the time to review an inventory of your skills, talents and strengths.

1._____ 2._____ 3 ._____ 4._____ 5._____

After you have used your own self-awareness 'mirror' then buy the *Strengths Finder* book. The book also provides a unique access code for the online questionnaire. The online questionnaire will take approximately one hour to complete all the questions and retrieve the results. Based on your answers to a number of questions the online program will then advise you of your top 5 strengths. After completing the test you will be surprised how aligned the results are to the 5 key strengths that you 'discovered' yourself. You will be pleased that your key strengths have been confirmed and revealed. The book and accompanying online profiling tool will give you fresh insight into your strengths and how to apply them to your life.

The *Strengths Finders* book says, "You can't fail a Strengths Finder because every signature theme contains the promise of a strength." [1] The questionnaire developed by Gallup helps you to discover your key strengths. I found it particularly helpful because you can progress through your career not knowing what you are good at and where you need to pay particular attention. The Strength Finders profiling method helps you 'Name' and 'Claim' your strengths. At the end of the test you also receive a 18 page analysis of your five key strengths.

- If you find there is an area of your life where you are not so proficient or you lack a key skill then look for other tools, techniques or people to assist you.
- Do not spend vast amounts of your time trying to be good at something where you will never be competent.
- There are no such things as weaknesses, just strengths that are lower down the ranking.
- Don't spend a lot of time on these areas, but understand that you may have to work on them if you have a job or role where these key skills are required.

- Your focus should be to develop your strengths and make them stronger. This is where you excel and this is where you will have the X-Factor that makes you stand out from others in your department, team, office or company.

For example, your key themes or strengths may be *Analytical, Intellection* (you like mental activity) and *Ideation* (you like to think up new ideas). These are excellent themes for a role in Marketing, R&D or new technology; however, they may not be a good fit for roles in government, banking or other sectors where there are clear policies, procedures and that are highly legislative. This may stifle your thoughts and idea creation and you would not be happy and fulfilled in this role. Conversely, if your key themes are *Empathy, Fairness* and *Harmony* then you may consider a role as a teacher, administrator, customer -facing role or job in the leisure industry. These may be professions where you can work more to your strengths.

Align to Your Strengths

You can work hard to improve the themes where you are not so strong but you may spend many long hours and a lot of energy trying to accomplish it and never succeed. Focus primarily on your strengths and look for the part of your life and job where you can use them.

I would suggest that you can't change your key strengths; these are deep in your character and will not change dramatically over time. Just like our marathon runner you will become frustrated and lose confidence if you cannot perfect and hone your God-given skills. Focus on what you are good at and you will get to the top of Maslow's pyramid.

Watch Outs

Once you have discovered your key themes you can now focus on improving them; however, you need to be careful. Sometimes you can be too good at something, you could use your strength too much that it becomes a weakness. I call them 'Watch Outs.' Yes, it sounds crazy, but a strength overdone will then become a Watch Out.

For example, a revolutions counter in a car. When the rpm (revs per minute) are between 2000 and 4000 then the power of the engine is at the maximum. If the accelerator/gas is pressed and you do not change gear then the rev counter starts to go to the red, when you hit the red then you are in the 'Watch Out' area. You have the same engine in the car but the strength is now overdone and you are in the red zone. You should focus more attention to your strengths that are overdone than your weaker areas. Strengths overdone can be much deadlier to your long-term job or career.

For example, one of your strengths may be *Harmony*, you like to agree with people and have agreement in a group, you like it when everyone is in one accord. You do not like conflict and will do what it takes for an easy life and avoid the confrontation and bad feelings. This can be a great strength in some situations when a peacemaker or arbitrator is required; however, this strength can be overdone when you desire that everyone is happy. In a work place situation, there will always be disagreement and conflict. People have different opinions and, in a high -achieving team, disagreement can sometimes be good. Always understand that it is not your role to get involved and to always arbitrate and make the peace in all situations. If you understand this strength and accompanying Watch Out then you will be careful with getting involved in arguments and areas that are of no concern to you. Play to your strength but do not overdo it.

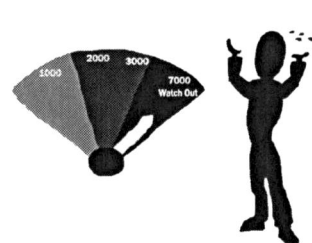

Another example is *Empathy*. Empathy is when you can understand people's feelings. You can relate to them, you can align with their emotions; you see the world through their eyes and see where they are coming from. In a corporate setting, it is good to have empathy; this is part of a strong EQ (see chapter 8). However, there is a Watch Out here. If you are too empathetic with your staff, you may not push and drive them to achieve. You may think you are pushing them too hard, you may understand that they need to be home with their family or out socializing with friends. These reasons are admirable and most team leaders or managers in this situation may agree; however, too much empathy and less focus on delivery results for the company will result in an ineffective and dysfunctional team. You will end up turning your department into a 'Country Club.' [4]

Name and Claim

After you have found your strengths and verified them with family and friends, this will give you much more confidence. You are starting to climb the Maslow pyramid to Self -Actualization. Display your Top 5 strengths in your office, keep them in your wallet, or enter them into your Smartphone and focus on them. As you continue your daily job or routine you are now more conscious of where you are working to your strengths and where you are overdoing a strength and making it a Watch Out. These are your unique strengths. There is no one else like you.

Other Personality Profiling Tools

There are many other personality-profiling tools on the market. Some include;

- Thomas-Kilmann Conflict Mode Instrument
- Hay Group Influence Strategies
- Hardiness Institute Hardisurvey
- III-R, Hirsh and Kummerow TYPE and Organizations
- Schnell and Hammer FIRO-B
- Belbin's Self Perception Inventory

- Blanchard's Leader Behaviour Analysis II,
- Hogrefe Manchester Personality,
- Hogrefe NEO Personal Insight,

Your career advisor, recruitment consultant, employment agency or your Human Resources (HR) department can assist you to identify other resources if you require them. There are also many online. I mention some of the others here for completeness in the event that you wish to use another profiling tool; however, the Strengths Finder is the simplest and provides quick and actionable steps.

Over many years I have taken many personality profiling tests and numerous 360 -degree feedback tests. Some of these tests are very costly, complex and take a long time to complete and receive the full feedback. The Strengths Finder test is simple and effective. It is also the most cost effective and the most accurate that will truly reflect your character. At the time of writing, the online test can be purchased for under $10. (Visit www.x4gy.com)

When your report is sent to you, read it over carefully. If you lack self-confidence, then by Naming and Claiming your strengths you will understand that you have skills and talents in areas that others do not have. It will give you added confidence as you work to your strengths and support any areas that you are not so strong in.

Before taking the online test, it is worthwhile to read the book. There are 34 themes described in detail; as you read the book select the ones that best fit your character and write them below.

1._____ 2._____ 3 ._____ 4._____ 5._____

Now you can complete the online test and see how well you did. Write these below. Did your strengths from the questionnaire align with the strengths you indicated above? Did they align with your first thoughts early in the chapter?

1._____ 2._____ 3 ._____ 4._____ 5._____

Firstly, it is critical that you understand your strengths. You cannot lead yourself and in turn lead others until you understand yourself first. You need to understand not only yourself but how you can use these unique strengths to lead others effectively. (See Chapter 6).

Mike Abrashaft puts it well in his book, *It's Your Ship*,

"Leaders must understand themselves first before they can lead others." [4]

If you have a coach, mentor or close friend then ask them to review your key themes with you. This will give you additional insight into your character. You could also share the report with your colleagues or manager. This will provide them valuable insight into how to engage and work with you in a more productive way.

A Few Dollars More

Everyone's style is different. Yes, by all means, take the good parts you observe from other leaders that you see and admire, but understand that we are all different and it is only by understanding your own personal strengths and applying them correctly and consistently that you will be fulfilled in your role or job.

In October 2008, I completed the Strengths Finder test for the first time. I was amazed at the results. I then repeated the test exactly five years later. The results were remarkably similar. Two of my top three strengths remained the same, underlying that these are my key strengths and were still strong 5 years later. There were also two themes that I had consistently overdone: *Responsibility* and *Restorative*. I consistently took responsibility for tasks and areas that were not my concern and with the addition of the Restorative theme, I tried to 'fix' everything around me. If a process, task, or job was broken or something needed to be fixed then I took responsibility for it. These strengths got me in trouble on more than one occasion. It is good to have a friend or partner that understands you. My wife delighted in taking every opportunity to remind me when I was overdoing my strengths! Over 5 years I had worked on these 2 key strengths to control them better. The 2 themes that I had frequently overdone,

Responsibility and *Restorative,* had now dropped from my top 5.

My strengths have not varied dramatically but only some have become more prominent. For sure, it was a good exercise and well worth the time. In a little over one hour and a few more dollars the test was completed, the report generated, action steps defined and I am on my way to setting targets and goals for my next stage of my life-long learning process.

As Lisa Nichols said when being interview by Raymond Aaron,

"No-one does me better than me."

Remember, there is only one person like 'you,' be the best 'you' on the planet. These key strengths form your unique brand. Your brand reflects who you are and what you stand for.

Do not try to be like someone else; you will fail miserably. Know your strengths, follow your long-term goals and be the best you can be.

In closing, Les Brown says it well,

"You don't have to be great to get started, but you do need to get started to be great."

So get started with discovering your strengths.

X Factors

- Identify your 5 Key Strengths through your own self analysis
- Take the Strengths Finder test
- Name and Claim your strengths
- Develop your awareness of how your Strengths can become Watch Outs
- Be the best you can be. Your key strengths reflect your unique brand. (more in Chapter 2)

Chapter 2

Develop Your Personal Brand

"To be in business today, our most important job is to be head marketer for the brand called You."

– Tom Peters

Introduction

Keith Ferrazzi, marketing and sales specialist, calls it 'Personal Message.' James Lafferty, CEO of British American Tobacco calls it 'Your Brand Equity.' Facebook calls it your 'Profile' and Raymond Aaron, author and marketer, says that 'Branding is the promises you make and the promises you keep.' Whatever you prefer to call it, your brand is now critical to your success in employment and business.

Marketing and branding are not just the bastions of small businesses and large corporations. Businesses spend millions developing and maintaining their brands. Their brand image is critical in today's marketplace. It is easier to sell products and services if your brand reflects what you are, your values and what you stand for.

The concept of personal branding is not new; it was first introduced in 1937 in the book *Think and Grow Rich* by Napoleon Hill. Hill describes,

"The new *brand* of leadership ……. will find abundant opportunity to lead in any walk of life. The depression was prolonged, largely, because the world lacked leadership of the new *brand*." [3]

Branding is the practice of creating an image of yourself based on your values, technical ability, clothes and physical appearance. The purpose is to develop a brand that will assist your job and career.

We all have personal brands. If this is a difficult concept for you to understand then think about some famous personalities. Oprah Winfrey, the richest presenter in the world, has branded herself as open, honest and a philanthropist. Consider also your favorite actors; some are very careful about protecting their brand and image. Benedict Cumberbatch, Jennifer Aniston and Anne Hathaway have reputations for excellent acting and leading parts in many blockbuster movies. If you hear they are acting in a new movie then you may arrange to see the movie even though you know nothing about the movie. You will buy into their brand before you buy into the product. Also consider Charlie Sheen or Tiger Woods. Both have brands that have been damaged and may take years to rebuild.

Personal Branding

As a professional and individual the same is also true. You should develop your particular brand image and work hard to protect it just like the movie stars and big businesses.

Are you going to be someone that is always prompt and on time? Will you focus on quality of your tasks and assignments? Will you be known as:

- The Technology person
- The Reports person
- The Presentations person
- The Fixer
- The Achiever
- The Visionary

Find your niche, develop it and stick to it. If you cannot find a niche then find what you are good at, develop that and make this your brand. In marketing, similar products are differentiated only by branding. Sometimes inferior products in terms of quality, service or delivery are preferred in favor of better quality products only because the branding and marketing of the inferior product is so much better. Sounds crazy but it is true. Many people buy brands first and then look to the product. The product needs to have a basic level of quality expected by the customer; however, all things being equal, the marketing and branding of the product will be the differentiator.

Raymond Aaron describes it well in his book, *Branding Small Business for Dummies*,

"Branding is the promises you make and the promises you keep. If you are always late, that's your brand." [5]

Be the only person in the office that dresses smart. Be the first person in the office and always on time. Do something slightly different to differentiate yourself from others.

The Halo Effect

If you have a secure and unique brand then this can provide you some grace and tolerance with others. Think about the Technology Person; they are brilliant with new technology, the latest Smartphones and gadgets are not a technical challenge to them. There is nothing they can't setup, configure or fix when it comes to technology. They have branded themselves as The Technology Person, probably unintentionally. They may be difficult to deal with; they may be obnoxious, impolite and rude. Their EQ is shocking and they upset everyone they meet. Their superiors keep them in the 'back office,' away from their colleagues and the general public; however, their manager tolerates their poor behavior because they have an outstanding brand. They can resolve every technical problem or challenge they are faced with. They have the Halo Effect that protects them because they have branded themselves as the Technology Person. They need to protect their brand, they need to stay at the forefront of technology and understand it intimately. If someone asks them to resolve a technical problem and they can't do it because they don't understand the technology or have not kept pace with the changes, then their brand is tarnished, their halo will slip and they will no longer have protection from all those annoying things that people dislike about them. Their job will be short and they may be fired.

As Dave Patten says in his book, *How to Market your Business*,

"Establishing a strong brand identify will take years, but you have to start somewhere." [6]

Online Brand Equity

Your personal brand is your brand equity in your workplace and social circles. This is where you market your product, which is 'You.' Dave Evens in his book, *Social Media Marketing*, describes it like this,

"Marketing – the thing that most of us do every day – has its roots in the word-of-mouth conversations that have linked buyers and sellers over the past few thousand years. Reputations were built based on experience." [7]

Now Marketing has moved from social meetings and interactions to the internet and social media. Social media is now being exploited to sell goods and services and of course '*You.*' Many of you have Facebook, LinkedIn, Xing or other social media exposure. Your brand and '*your stuff*' are now online for all to see. Facebook has over 1 billion users and therefore your brand could be theoretically viewed by 1 in 7 people on the planet! Your future employer, current employer and also current and future friends will for sure want to view your profile.

Les Brown made a very compelling point while in Amsterdam during a National Achievers Congress. He said,

"90% of those who will help you with your dreams are still strangers to you." [8]

These strangers are the people you need in your future job role, career or business venture. These people will see your brand and profile online before you ever meet them and get a chance to make a first impression. The old cliché, 'you don't get a <u>second</u> chance to make a <u>first</u> impression' is not true anymore; it is now 'you don't get a <u>first</u> chance to make the <u>first</u> impression', at least in the physical world. You don't have the luxury anymore to smarten up, put on a nice suit and smile to create a good first impression. It is now too late; the impression has been made, good or bad - online. The decision to employ you or work with you has already been made based on your online profile.

Jealously protect your online profile, do not post inappropriate photos of you and your friends and don't post profanities. Be mindful of the comments your friends post; you are branded with your friends by association, one of the most powerful branding techniques that companies use. Your profile, your groups and friends are all now in the public domain. As a rule, re-read everything before you click 'Post,' 'Like,' or comment.

A prospective employer, friend, partner or business partner can and will view your profile and determine if they want to do business with you long before they make the initial contact. Your brand needs to match their expectations; these are your customers, <u>you are now the product</u>.

Offline Brand Equity in the Corporate World

Your reputation at your place of work is mainly based on personal contact and conversations with individuals. While social networking has its place it is rarely exploited in the workplace to locate and network with colleagues within the organization. Some large and enlightened companies may have an internal HR system to profile employees and allow them to locate each other; however, they may focus on HR performance metrics and development and not personal or social profiles. Reputations, trust and experience are gained through casual conversations, personal meetings and other social interactions between individuals.

In an office environment your brand can now be managed and controlled. Guys, you can make a decision whether you shave or adopt the rough and ready look. Your personal grooming and dress code can be established before you get to your office or workplace. You can control your appearance, body language and how you interact with others and exploit a high EQ (See Chapter 8). You determine when you come to the office, your interactions with others and when you leave. This freedom is not available to you online.

Protect Your Brand Equity

Protect your brand. If you have established yourself as someone who is always prompt and on time for meetings then protect this at all costs. If you are going to be late then make sure you have a very good reason. Repeatedly arriving a few minutes late for every meeting will damage your brand. When you have a reputation for being late it is extremely difficult to remove this perception from the minds of others.

Your work colleagues find comfort in knowing that you are reliable and, of course, repeatable. They can rely on you if they require an assignment or task completed on time. They will have confidence in your brand and come back to you for these time-critical tasks.

Dave Patten in his book, *How to Market your Business*, explains it like this,

"You must constantly be striving to think up fresh ways of adding value, tuning the service, improving the range and getting closer to the customer's needs. One of the hardest tasks in marketing is to make sure that you are remembered." [6]

In a social and business setting, make sure you are remembered for the right reasons.

The Seven Second Rule

Ask yourself, "What business am I in? Why? From this you can establish your brand. This is the first thing people see. People buy brands before they buy products. How many of you will plan to buy the latest cool and innovative Apple product? Even if you have never seen it! You buy the Apple brand first; you know it will be innovative, well-designed and cool. This is the same in business. If your personal brand is The Smart One, you always dress well and are well-groomed and presented. People will see this first. Your professionalism and credibility are assessed within **7 seconds** of meeting someone. [9] This is people's first impression of you. During the next **4 minutes** they will get to know you better and establish if your personal brand is good and that they want to do business with you or go elsewhere. Important research during informal encounters at parties, clubs and casual meetings was conducted by New York psychiatrist, Dr. Leonard Zunin. He concludes,

"The first four minutes is the key to establishing lasting social relationships, family harmony, business success and sexual pleasure. During this brief period there is insufficient time to impress with the spoken word. Virtually all the information exchanged is by means of silent speech. Research has also shown that once we come to a judgment about whether or not we like the other person this conclusion is resistant to change. Rather than alter our opinion we distort incoming information in a way that makes it support our initial assumption." [10]

Your presentation, clothing and body language are the first things that people see and the last things they will remember. After the encounter, your personality and clothing will be remembered long after the subject of your conversation.

Where Are You on the Ladder?

Raymond Aaron in his book, *Branding Small Business for Dummies*, describes the Branding Ladder. He says that,

"97% of businesses live on the first rung of the ladder '**Brand Absence.**' They earn less than they want to earn, far less than they should earn and far less than they would earn if they did exactly the same work under a real brand." [5]

Individuals are no different than a business. Brand yourself in line with the work or role you have. Identify your role and develop a Unique Selling Point (USP) that will differentiate you in the eyes of others and your manager. This is **Brand Awareness**. The USP has to be appropriate. A machine operator in a factory that wears a suit to work may look smart; however, he will brand himself wrongly given his job role and areas of responsibility. He could brand himself as always being on time and working late to finish an important task. In this environment, like many others, you don't have to do much more to be noticed, go the extra mile. As the saying goes 'there are no traffic jams on the extra mile.'

The third rung of the ladder is **Brand Preference**. Team leaders, department managers or colleagues will come to you because they

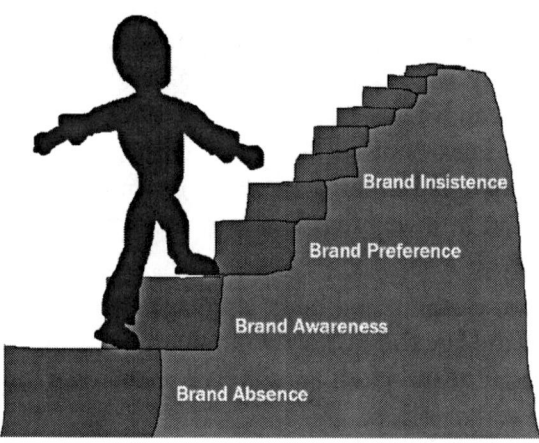

prefer to work with you instead of others. They know you will finish the task on time and they don't need to follow up. They know that the quality will be good and they will not need to come back for repeated changes. Of course, like all good things, this can be overdone and people repeatedly come to you because you say yes. You are then overloaded and become ineffective. This is a Watch Out. (See Chapter 1) You may slip with quality or timely delivery and your brand becomes tarnished. Protect the brand and explain that you cannot take on additional workload at the moment.

The best step on the ladder is **Brand Insistence.** Have you ever noticed that your manager or team leader always goes to the one person for a particular job? Think of The Results Person. You give him a tough project, it touches a large part of the organization, requires EQ, diplomacy but strength of character to push through a change in the organization. The manager knows who to approach for such a job, The Results Person. He gets the job done, will push through change and rarely needs to come back for direction or guidance. Give him the task and point him in the correct direction then watch out. The Results Person has Brand Insistence. The manager will insist on The Results Person because he gets jobs done. Even if The Results Person is transferred to another part of the company then he may be called back because he has the brand and reputation to get things done. When you get to this level then you have made it. You are branded and people will insist on using you. Your career will progress to bigger and better challenges.

Consider the Customer

The fundamentals of building your brand are described in Raymond Aaron's book.

"Know what your customer really wants and expects. Find out what your supervisor or manager requires of you, when does he want the assignment completed, the level of quality and end deliverable. Do what you say you will, over deliver every task and every time. Remember what you do is more important that what you say." [5]

Consider the customer, in this case your managers' entire experience. Are you easy to do business with? Treat others as you would want to be treated yourself. A strong EQ and empathy for others will help you understand their point of view.

Live your brand every day. Do not let your guard down. If you are known for always dressing smart then be careful on the 'dress down Friday.' Do not wear something totally inappropriate that will damage your brand.

Be consistent from Monday morning at 9am through Friday night at 5pm. People like a clear, determined and consistent brand.

X Factors

- Personal Branding – You are now the Product
- Develop your Brand and Unique Selling Point
- Protect your online Brand
- Protect your physical Brand
- Climb the Ladder to Brand Insistence and achieve your goals (more in Chapter 3)

Chapter 3

Goal Setting

"There is no hope of success for the person who does not have a central purpose or definitive goal."

                                                  – Napoleon Hill

Introduction

Your purpose in life involves having a dream or, in Napoleon Hill's words, a *definitive goal*. Before you can do anything you have to know what it is that you want to achieve. Otherwise, why bother? Most people who are not goal driven have no idea what it is they want to achieve, but once you focus on your dreams you can break down your purpose and passion into manageable steps. These will allow you to advance towards realizing those dreams. Those steps are known as goals and the goals need to be short-term, medium-term and long-term. How can you hope to achieve anything if you do not even know what it is that you want? You therefore should consider your purpose and passion before you even begin the process of setting goals.

The potter must consider first what he wants to create and have the finished art form in his mind or on sketch before he can start to discover his creation within the clay. The same is true for the sculpture and his marble, the mason with his stone and the artist with his paint and canvas.

Michelangelo puts it succinctly,

"Every block of stone has a statue inside it and it is the task of the sculptor to discover it."

The most valuable resources on our planet are not the unmined diamonds of South Africa, not the undrilled oil of Texas, but the untapped potential of people. Their unlived dreams, unachieved goals, unused skills, undeveloped talents and undisclosed ideas are the valuable resources of this generation that we should unlock and unleash. We all have a statue inside of us ready to be discovered. (Expanded from an original thought by Les Brown) [8]

Helen Keller, American author and political activist, at the age of 19 months suffered an illness that left her both deaf and blind. She was asked if there was anything worse than being blind. Her reply was,

"The only thing worse than being blind is having sight but no vision."

What is your vision for the future? What dreams, passions and desires are within your heart waiting to be discovered?

Napoleon Hill in his book, *Outwitting the Devil*, puts it like this,

"The first thing you will notice about a drifter is his total lack of a major purpose in his life." [11]

Hill goes on to describe the non-drifter,

"He is always engaged in doing something definite, through some well-organized plan which is definite. He has a major goal in life toward which he is always working and many minor goals, all of which lead toward his central scheme." [11]

Keller calls it *vision*, Hill refers to it as *central scheme* and I name it your *Purpose*.

Your Purpose

What is your purpose in your life? Socially, with family, spiritually, within your career, hobby or other vocation you have in life? What will give you fulfillment and self-actualization? It is not within the scope of this book to ask the question - Why are you here? However it is important to reflect on why you have been placed on this earth. If you have faith in a higher power then your purpose may be clearer, if not, then you should search for your purpose, without this it is difficult to live a life of fulfillment. When you have reached the end of your life what events, people or lessons will go through your mind? Will you say, "I wish I had spent more time at work, more time with family, more time cultivating relationships, building my business to be bigger or better?" Try to picture yourself in this position and look back. What will be your main thought? This will get you closer to your purpose, your dreams and vision for your life. You will start to see the art form appearing from within your clay.

You could ask yourself the question; do you always look forward to 5pm when work finishes? Why? Is it to meet friends, complete a personal project, a special activity, work with a voluntary organization or church, or perhaps a particular sport or hobby? This is where your purpose could lie.

Here are a few questions to ask yourself to help you make a first impression on your clay:

- What is your purpose in life?
- What is your passion? What floats your boat? Excites you?
- What does a long-term plan look like for your life?
- If you had unlimited time and resources what would you want to do?
- What would you like people to say about you when you have gone?

Personal Vision Statement

Write a clear and overriding statement. It should be short and memorable, like a vision or mission statement. E.g. 'By the time I am 65 I wish to be retired and living in Italy with a small property business providing me with passive income to enjoy work, rest and play.' Remember Hill's words,

"Even weak plans have a way of becoming strong if definitely applied." [11]

It may not be easy but do your best to write something.

_____

_____

_____

Your Passion

What is your passion in life? It could be something you do socially with friends, your church or other voluntary group you are involved with, a hobby or activity, or your work or vocation. Some people define themselves by the job they do. When you meet someone socially you ask, 'What do you do?' The reply may be, "I work in a bank," "I am an engineer," or "I am a builder." Many times our job defines us, gives us a sense of being and a sense of belonging. In some cases this is okay; however, it may not be your passion. When you wake in the morning, what is the first thing you think about? What is the last thing you focus on before you sleep? When you are at work, do you focus on the weekend, being with friends or taking part in a sport or other activity? What do you live for? Do you enjoy your 9-5 job? Is this your passion? It is important to understand this. Ask yourself, would you do your current job even if you were not paid to do it?

Donald Trump, American business magnate, has personified the words of Napoleon Hill,

"It is actually no harder to think big as it was to think small." [11]

Trump is renowned for being ambitious. He has big plans for his real-estate projects in New York City; he has clear and concise goals and a vision for what he wants to build. He creates the blueprint and realizes his dreams. His purpose and passion are clear. Hill also describes people's universal weakness as a lack of ambition.

It is important to find your passion early in your life and career. If you find it early, you can live a life of fulfillment and excitement rather than repeating your same life day in and day out in the same job until you are fired or retire.

Your Persistence

Are you persistent? Will you follow through on a plan and persevere until it is completed? Will you hold yourself accountable to achieve a goal? Will you forsake your personal time, comfort and short-term gain to reach a lifetime goal? We live in a world where we want instant levels of service and instant gratification and fulfillment. We want everything yesterday. Will you delay gratification in the short-term and be persistent to achieve your goals. Every day you should make small incremental steps to your goals. Look at your daily agenda or to-do list. Does the list reflect your long-term goals? Are these tasks taking you one-step closure to your goals or one-step further away? Your daily routine and tasks will determine where you will be in 5 years time. It is the principal described in Jeff Olson's book The Slight Edge.

"That the things you do every single day, the things that don't look dramatic, that don't even look like they matter, do matter." [12]

Your Plan

Start with your final purpose and passion and work back to the current day. What would be a perfect day look like to you? Where would you spend that day? Who would you spend it with? Do you dream of sitting on a beach drinking tequila with your 16 grandchildren playing on the beach? This would be a dream for some but a nightmare for others. Would you like to be the head of your organization, voluntary group or social circle? Do you seek to pursue money and wealth, respect or status? Do you want fulfillment by giving something back to your family, community or world? What do you want to achieve? How do you measure your achievement? And how do you know when you will get there?

The successful leader must plan his work and work the plan, as the saying goes, failing to plan is planning to fail. Hill in his book 'Think and Grow Rich' cites 30 major causes of failure. High on the list at number 2 is a lack of a well-defined purpose in life. He goes on to says,

"There is no hope of success for the person who does not have a central purpose, or definitive goal at which to aim." [3]

98% of those he analyzed had no such aim. Perhaps this was the major cause of their failure.

Stretch Goals

Dave Ramsay, Personal Finance Educator says,

"Goals that flow from vision will make you hurt yourself trying to achieve them." [13]

Consider your goals carefully; do not make them too easy. Consider some stretch goals. This is a goal just beyond your current reality and where you feel un-comfortable. If you are growing, you will always be out of our comfort zone. The magic happens when we get out of our comfort zone and learn new skills.

Michelangelo said,

"The greater danger for most of us lies not in setting our aim too high and falling short; but in setting our aim too low and achieving our mark."

Long Term Goals

We start with long-term goals because without a destination in mind we will wander aimlessly and achieve nothing. Dave Ramsay says,

"A vision motivates you beyond yourself." [13]

Your vision will pull you up, drive you and motivate you. If you do not know what you want to achieve then how can you even begin to think about the details of how you will get there?

We begin with our purpose and passion to enable us to identify the long-term goals. Maybe you are passionate to teach and impart knowledge to others. A long-term goal might be to become a college professor. Of course different objectives may be to become a coach or a pastor. These are different vocations in life but they all fall within the same passion; to give back, educate and develop others.

Take your passion and think of a few different long-term goals of how you wish to realize that passion. Don't consider the HOW part of this yet, that comes later, we want to address the WHY first. For now you are forming the image of what is in your clay. Once you have selected a long term goal or goals you will need to ask yourself why you want to achieve this goal and how it helps you realize your long term purpose and passion.

This will help you build a long-term plan for your life. As you begin to mold your desires you will find that some goals are a better fit for your purpose compared to other goals. You will want to narrow those goals down to a manageable select number of goals and then use those goals to give yourself additional focus as you begin to look at medium and short term goals.

When you have selected your goal, you will want to ask yourself what it will take to realize that particular goal. For example, if you want to become a basketball coach you will want to know how to play basketball and know the rules for the game. Ideally you will want to have at least a small degree of talent. Knowing these steps will help you to develop the stages that you will need to achieve your goal.

Defining Your Long Term Goals

In this part of the exercise you will want to ask yourself:
- What is my purpose and passion?
- What are three Long Term goals that will help me realize this purpose?
- How can I use my passion?
- What will it take to realize this goal?

Long-Term Goal 1 _____

Long-Term Goal 2 _____

Long-Term Goal 3 _____

Medium-Term Goals

One nice aspect about the medium goals is that they will become the milestones by which you will measure your progress. Each time you achieve a medium goal, you will be able to congratulate yourself on passing a milestone marker towards achieving your long-term goal. Medium goals typically have a 2 – 5 years time span. Numerous goals can be worked concurrently as well. This means that you can learn to play basketball while taking a class on leadership and finding a coaching position! If your passion is within your company or industrial sector then you need to plan your career. Most forward thinking companies will have a formal career succession planning process. If you want to climb the corporate ladder, make sure you talk to your manager and show that you want to step up to a more senior role. Make sure you are on the succession plan and you know what skills and behaviors you need to attain before you can move to the next role.

With a proper plan, when the opportunity arises you will be ready. Luck is where opportunity meets preparation. Create a plan; break the long-term goal into smaller tasks that can be achieved in a 2-5 years time scale.

In this step you will want to ask yourself:

• What are my 2-5 year goals in the areas of job, career, business and financial?

- What are my goals in the areas of health, family, friends, relation-ship and education?
- What goals should I do first?
- What goals can be worked concurrently?
- How will I measure my progress?
- How will I know when I get there?

Medium-Term Goal 1 _____

Medium-Term Goal 2 _____

Medium-Term Goal 3 _____

Medium-Term Goal 4 _____

Medium-Term Goal 5 _____

Short-Term Goals

These goals are the monthly or quarterly steps that you will take to achieve the medium goals. Essentially you are now going to take the medium goals and break them down into the small monthly activities that you need to achieve the medium goals. For example, if you want to learn a new skill you would first need to identify colleges, training programs, seminars or online training programs.

The key to making short-term goals is that they need to be Specific, Measurable, Achievable, Realistic and Time-Bound. This is known as a SMART.

Lastly you will want to make sure your goals can be achieved in a timely fashion. Short-term goals should be a maximum of one year, but I like to break them down into 4 quarterly increments. This allows me to measure my progress and reevaluate my goals against the SMART formula to make sure that these goals can be achieved.

Throughout this process you should check your short-term goals against the following list:

- Do my goals follow the SMART formula?
- Are all my short-term goals aligned to my medium-term goals?

Short-Term Goal Quarter 1 _____

Short-Term Goal Quarter 2 _____

Short-Term Goal Quarter 3 _____

Short-Term Goal Quarter 4 _____

Self-Talk

Have you ever been motivated by a speaker, debate or discussion, a sermon or lecture? Words spoken to us audibly can motivate us to do something greater, better and beyond ourselves. A great orator can drive us to new levels of achievement. Have you considered not only the words you hear but the words you say to yourself? Do these words also inspire you to achieve and drive you to succeed in a task or goal? Probably not, be careful of your self-talk. Les Brown, the motivational speaker says that 87% of your self-talk is negative. Focus your thoughts on positive things, what you are good at, where you excel, your successes and small incremental wins. You will reach your goals one step at a time. Remember,

"Our only limitations are those we set up in our minds." [3]

John Maxwell is his book, *Sometimes You Win Sometimes You Learn*, writes,

"The most important person you ever talk to is yourself, so be careful what you say." [14]

Daily Focus

Read your personal vision statement 1-2 times per day. Read it as you dress in the morning, after your prayer time or as you prepare for bed. If you are a visual learner then create a picture or vision board of your vision. Cut out pictures of your dream location, house, boat, family and paste them on a board. You can focus on this. Your body will only go where you mind has been several times before. Convince your mind that you have already achieved your goal. Use a vision board and ongoing goal setting and make it part of your daily experience.

"Anything the human mind can believe, the human mind can achieve." [3]

Remember there are no limitations in your mind; anything is possible as long as you focus on it.

Attention

Achieving our goals is one of the most rewarding things we can do for ourselves. T. Harv Ecker tells us,

"Where attention goes, energy flows and results shows." [15]

So let us start by giving our goals that very needed attention. Do not just look at your current situation (job, no job, career, hobbies and skills); rather, look instead towards your long-term purpose and passion.

Determine what you will sacrifice to attain this goal, will you give up your time, talents or treasures to achieve your long-term objective and take short-term pain for long-term gain.

X Factors

- You have identified your passion and your WHY?
- You have a personal vision statement, 20-30 years.
- You have defined your medium-term goals, 2-5 years.
- You have defined your short-term goals for this year.
- You are motivated to keep your goals.
- Your Self Talk should be positive.

Chapter 4

Life Long Learning

"See what a person is doing every day, day after day and you'll know what that person is and what he or she is becoming"

– John Maxwell

Introduction

In the formal education system, (schools, colleges and universities) you get the lesson first and then the test at the end. In real life, the world is much tougher. In life you get the test first and then the lessons come after. However, the lesson only comes if you sit and reflect on the test and how you can improve for the future. As John Maxwell says that in life,

"It's going to sting, it's going to hurt …… Learning isn't something that stops when we are handed a diploma. In fact, that is actually the point when the real learning begins. The lessons we are given in school are not the things that carry us through life; those are just the lessons that give us the basic tools to face the world outside of the classroom walls." [15]

Napoleon Hill has a tougher message regarding the American school system in 1938,

"The schools and colleges teach practically everything except the principals of individual achievement. They require young men and women to spend from four to eight years acquiring abstract knowledge, but do not teach them what to do with this knowledge after they get it." [11]

Thankfully the teaching in schools, colleges and universities has improved greatly since 1938 however we must remember that after we leave university with our new degree our education and learning processes are just beginning. The process of learning and growing should continue long after we have left the formal education system. It is our personal responsibility to continue learning in our personal and work related experiences. This should never stop. Ask yourself, how am I developing? Am I the same person last year as I am today? In one year's time, how can I change?

It is Your Responsibility

If you are fortunate to have a job and a good career it is not the role of your manager and Human Resources (HR) department to organize your training and development. The responsibility lies with you. A good forward thinking company will encourage you to consider your holistic educational needs. They will propose a mix of experiential training, work assignment, a coach or a mentor. Formal training courses will also form part of this training. Although the HR department can help you, the ultimate responsibility for your ongoing education remains with you.

Ask yourself, why should your employer pay for expensive training courses to train you in the latest tools and techniques to ensure your stay at the forefront of your profession and career if you are not prepared to make a similar investment in time, money and other resources yourself? A sobering question.

Develop yourself, find courses, seminars and conferences that will improve your knowledge, either in your current field of employment, in a new area where you wish to develop or something that is unrelated to your work but related to your long-term goals. Some employers may finance suitable courses or provide additional vacation time or leave if they relate to your job roles or areas of responsibility. If they don't then this should not stop you from investing in yourself. Many successful individuals spend a large percentage of their time and money on courses to improve themselves. They see this as a personal investment in themselves to improve and develop.

Learn Life Lessons

Without reflecting on life's events, we will not really take time to learn and develop. Sometimes our failures teach us the hardest lessons. We lose our temper, forget to buy fuel or gas for our car or make a mistake at work. It is better to ask ourselves what we could have done differently to prevent the situation from occurring in the first place.

Lets recall Maxwell's words that life "is going to sting, it's going to hurt" but rather than wasting energy by attempting to make excuses or blaming others, we should calmly take a step back and learn from the experience. We do not want to invite problems by creating them ourselves, but we need to be prepared to face each problem as it presents itself. In doing so we will be able to face the challenges of our lives and grow to become a greater and better person. Evaluate, learn the lesson, internalize it and then move on.

As we face hardship we will develop and grow. We also have the opportunity to observe the struggles of others and learn from their example. An intelligent person learns from his mistakes but a wise person learns from others mistakes also.

"Successful leaders are learners. And the learning process is ongoing." [16]

Maxwell could not be more correct here because this is exactly what is being described. Struggles and hardships in life are fluid and always change. We cannot overcome one challenge and then think that every challenge will be the same after that. We cannot learn one tool or technique and apply this to every problem or challenge we face.

One Time Event or a Process

Major events in our lives are only a milestone, not a stop. For example to graduate from university is an event. To attend and complete a training course is an event. To attend a seminar is an event. This may punctuate your learning but it is not the process of learning. The process of learning starts when we are born and should never stop. Learning is a process of many events, seminars, trainings, reading and podcasts etc. There are numerous learning and educational materials available to us. Online course, CDs of great speakers, DVDs of key training materials, seminars, webinars, many of which are free, in abundance and are available to all. We are not short of access and availability of materials. If our intelligence and growth was based on the availability of materials then everyone would be much smarter and wiser, however this is not the case. Jeff Olson explains it well,

"If access to the right information were the answer, we'd all be rich, healthy, happy and fulfilled. And most of us are none of these things. The secret ingredient is your philosophy. The secret is to change the way you think.' 'To understand patience; to understand that little steps, compounded do make a difference. That the things you do every single day, the things that don't look dramatic, that don't even look like they matter, do matter." [12]

Olson thus explains to us the importance of the continuous learning process, every day, day after day. We will always have the chance to learn something new so that we are more prepared for what comes ahead. Knowing what resources to use will help us build our own plan for learning. Here are just a select number of resources to continue learning.

- **Books** – Select a personal development book (like this), or a book that teaches new skills required for your job, read a portion every day. You could ask a friend or colleague to read the same book and you could discuss and exchange notes. This active learning process will ensure that you remember and apply more of the learning's and lessons from the book. Anthony Robbins writes – *"Years ago I got hooked on a habit that turned out to be one of the most valuable of my life: reading at least 30 minutes a day. Jim Rohn, one of my teachers, told me that reading something of substance, something of value, something that was nourishing, something that taught you distinctions, was more important than eating. 'Miss a meal,' he said, "but don't miss your reading."* [17]

- **Audio Books** - If you don't have time to read then this is no excuse. Many books come in audio format. Some are abridged and don't have the full book content however learning the key lessons from a book are better than not reading anything.

- **Podcasts** – There are many educational podcasts available, many of these are free. Look for them on iTunes. There are podcasts on almost every subject you can imagine; Management, Sales, Marketing, Career development, Business, News, Investing, Language skills, improving your skills in IT, Photography, Personal finance, Yoga, the list is endless. There will be something available to help you grow and develop. Podcasts are excellent to listen to on the bus or train. Don't let a long commute to your work spoil your chance to learn, a long commute can be an opportunity to learn something new.

- **Seminars and Conferences** – There are many seminars available on varying subjects. Some of these address your specialist area or business sector. Software companies, trade organizations, chambers of commerce or other trade bodies may organize events for members and affiliates. When you are on their mailing list and attend one seminar or conference then they will pass (or sell) your details to other organizations, you will never be short of seminars and conferences to attend.

- **Webinars or Google+ Hangouts** – some trade organizations or special interest groups will hold webinars. These are online events with video and audio streaming. You will need to pre-register for these events. The URL/link and login information will be sent in advance and you then dial into the call at the pre-arranged time. Many of these companies will organize these free so there is no cost to you with the exception of having to listen to some marketing efforts before and after the call. You can also 'raise a hand' or ask a question online. Many property investment companies will organize webinars, also Strengths Finders, John Maxwell group, Raymond Aaron and many others are available. There will be something that works for you. It is another way of educating yourself for no cost apart for some of your personal time.

- **Online Courses** – There are an increasing number of online courses, these are called MOOCs, Massive Open Online Course, many universities have online courses open to the general public and many are free. They provide a high-level introduction to a course, if you are interested you provide your email address and personal information and you have access to the full online version. When you complete the course you then receive a certificate of completion.

- **YouTube** – You will find some great educational materials. TED talks are particularly educational. There are also a number of motivational interviews, videos and audio books by teachers such as Anthony Robbins, Zig Ziglar and John Maxwell. All have free training materials that can be viewed online.

- **Daily motivational quotes** - Sent to your email address are another great resource.

- **Daily video clips** – Can also be sent to your email address. You click on the URL and you have an instant one minute motivational video, perfect for when you are having lunch at your desk or while travelling on a bus or train.

- **Facebook** – Page feeds from your favorite authors, motivational speakers or professional trade bodies in your chosen field of expertise are also a good source of development and educational materials. You will also find out about other webinars and conferences through Facebook however, there are many marketing materials you need to avoid to find the good high value added materials.

"The mind is nothing more than the sum total of one's habits!" [11]

Make it your daily habit to learn. As Anthony Robbins was taught, it is better to skip a meal than skip your daily reading. Build an educational plan into you short and medium goals using some of the resources mentioned.

Transformation Learning

Transformational change in your character can occur at a training course or seminar. You have that light bulb moment where you learn something fundamental, which changes your thought, dream, attitudes or behaviors. The act of attending a seminar or conference is an event; however, you can turn this event into a transformational change if you make the decision to change your life. Anthony Robbins, Andy Harrington or Robert Kiyosaki seminars can have this effect. Their seminars challenge you to take control of your mental, emotional, physical and financial future. These seminars are not for everyone however, everyone can take something from them and apply the transformational change to your life.

There is a big difference between training and education. They sound similar however, training is a physical event. You may attend a course or shadow someone to learn a new skill. Education goes much deeper. It is change of mindset to learn a new skill or concept; you apply it to your mind and apply it to your life. It is an ongoing process. Training does not just include learning and applying new technical skills, it also extends to the world of sport. World class athletes know this very well.

The British world class athlete, Sebastian Coe, won four Olympic medals in 1980 and 1984. He understood the concept of ongoing training and personal development. During a speech at the National Achievers Congress in London in 2012, he said,

"Every morning you wake up to start your training knowing that somewhere in the world there is a competitor working hard to beat you." [18]

To an athlete at the top of their profession, they need to work harder and longer for 4 years to get the chance of beating their competitor. The world of the military is no different. Consider the following quote from Captain D. Michael Abrashoff, former commander of USS Benfold,

"Show me someone who has never made a mistake and I will show you someone who is not improving [himself] or organization." [4]

In the military you need to constantly train, develop and improve, there are no second chances when you go into battle with the enemy. One of you is not going home! This example is more acute however, it serves to illustrate that we should all develop and have a plan for our lifelong learning and development.

You need to constantly develop yourself to be the right person, in the right place at the right time. Don't wait for Lady Luck to help you learn the right thing. There is no such thing as luck. Luck is where opportunity meets preparation. Ensure you prepare your mind, body and skills to meet the job and career opportunities of the future. The world keeps turning and you need to improve and hone your technical skills for your job and career, your mental skills to manage people or skills of resilience to keep going when life gets tough. If you don't continue to learn the next wave of young graduates or athletes will take your position, job and end you career. You may also be outsourced or downsized as companies are forced to reduce costs.

Your Conditioning

Challenge your conditioning like the baby elephant that is tied to a wooden stake in the ground. The young elephant is too small to pull the stake out the ground and become free. After a while the young elephant gives up. When the elephant is older, larger and much

stronger it remembers that it could not break free of the wooden stake in the ground. Although the elephant can easily pull the stake and break free, its mental conditioning says that he cannot do it. This is where our own mind has been programmed and pre-conditioned against us.

Think of a situation where your friends and colleagues mindset have been pre-conditioned against you. They will say that a task cannot be done, that it is impossible, that they have tried it before and it didn't work, they have a friend of a friend that tried it and failed. These people can pull you back and stop you from doing something new in your life, learning a new skill, starting a new business, investing in something new. Consider the words that I heard recently. If your friends and family don't laugh at your goals then maybe they are not big enough! If you find that your friends are laughing too much at your ideas then rather than change your ideas, maybe you need to change your friends!

Consider the experiment about 5 monkeys in a cage. Although I don't condone experiments on animals, we can learn from this illustration. In the monkey cage was a ladder and at the top of the ladder was a banana. Each monkey in turn climbed the ladder and each monkey was sprayed with very cold water. One by one all 5 monkeys tried to climb the ladder to get the banana. Eventually the monkeys tried no longer, none tried to claim the 'prize'. One by one the orig-

inal monkeys in the cage were exchanged with new monkeys that had never experienced the spray of cold water. As the new monkey tried to climb the ladder the other original monkeys pulled it back to 'safety'. None of the monkeys dared to claim the banana. One by one all the original monkeys were replaced with new monkeys, at the end of the experiment none of the monkeys in the cage had experienced the spraying of the cold water yet none of them tried to eat the banana. Whenever one monkey tried to climb the ladder the others pulled him back! Whether this experiment ever took place, I am unsure; however, it is a good illustration about being pre-conditioned by those around you. You are the average of the 5 people you spend the most time with. Make sure that these 5 people are pulling you up and not dragging you down!

Think outside of the box, outside of your comfort zone; don't always listen to your friends if they are negative and trying to pull you back. The magic in your life happens when you are out of your comfort zone; this is where the growth is. When you are trying something new and expanding your mind, job or career. Out of your comfort zone is where your next challenge will be.

Alex Mandossian, online Marketer says,

"People fail because they don't do what's required or do it long enough." [19]

What is the crucial learning moments in your life? What are the key decisions or turning points in your life that have changed and shaped you? Use these events. Remember they are the milestones by which you can mark your progress. Far too often people think in the 'now'. They worry about their current discomfort or their anxiety. It is ultimately a journey that we must take. No one has ever promised the journey will be easy. Sometimes things will go smoothly in life. Other times things can be difficult. We must always remember to take the good days along with the bad days. Think about your long-term, medium-term and short-term goals in chapter 3. Set goals as an integral part of these plans.

Do you think like Richard Templar when he quipped,

"It's hard enough just getting through the day without trying to improve as well." [20]

Write a lifelong learning plan, share it with a friend, coach or mentor in order for them to keep you accountable. They will ensure you make your plan and stick to it.

X Factors

- Understand that your education is not a onetime event
- Decide to become a Life Long Learner
- Develop a plan to educate yourself
- Select the online and offline resources you will need to meet you learning goals
- Learn something new every day. Skip a meal if you must but do not skip learning. Organize your time schedule to accomplish this. (more in Chapter 5)

Chapter 5

Time Management

"Let him who would enjoy a good future waste none of his present."

-Roger Ward Babson

Introduction

In today's world we have more ability to communicate to people than we ever did before. We have more channels available to us through fixed telephone lines, mobile and smart phones, Facebook, Chat, Skype and numerous conferencing facilities, but have you considered that our work rate and productivity may in fact be decreasing. With the increasing introduction of technology there is more and more of an intrusion in our life. There can be multiple channels of communication open to you at any one time. This may distract you from your primary goals and objectives. In addition to the electronic communication available to us we also have interruptions from staff and colleagues all demanding our time.

You need to develop a strategy to focus on goals and objectives without becoming unduly distracted. For sure, if you are a senior manager or in Human Resources, people are your job, you should have an open door policy and be available for consultation. You should ensure that your staff and colleagues and your manager understand the best form of communication that you prefer and the style that maintains your efficiency. It is also important that you understand their favored communication style to maximize your time. E.g. do you prefer to have a daily or weekly meeting with colleagues and associates or do you prefer that they send a short email or quick text to communicate relevant information? If you are struggling with the multiple forms of communication and constant interruptions then your time may be slowly eroded, you lose your efficiency and at the end of each day you ask yourself 'Where did the day go?' This section will help you develop strategies to manage your time better. Of course you can't manage time, what you can manage is your priorities and how you use time effectively to accomplish your objectives and goals.

Make a Daily Log of Your Activity

Start by recording what you do throughout your day. At the very minimum, record every hour, but try to record in half hour blocks. I do not advise recording in more detail than that because it will become tedious and you will spend more time recording your routine than getting work done! By keeping a log of what you do throughout your day, you will be able to establish a baseline that will help you determine when you are most productive and where your time is lost.

When are you Most Productive?

Once you have a log, you will begin to notice patterns in your work day. Are you the most productive in the mornings, afternoons or evening? Does the time of your productivity change between different days of the week? It might be that you are most productive on Monday mornings and least productive on Wednesday afternoons. Sometimes people have trouble keeping focus after lunch or mid-morning. Is there a certain time of the day that you find yourself getting coffee repeatedly just to keep energy levels high? Look for patterns such as these as they will be helpful for the next step.

When are you least Productive?

Are you noticing that some parts of your day are not productive? Why might that be? Considering this can you develop strategies to maintain productivity during these periods. You may notice that you need an energy drink or extra coffee mid-morning to fight off some sleepiness if you feel drowsy in the middle of the morning. If you found that you have trouble focusing after lunch, then you may need to eat lunch at a different time of the day or smaller meals throughout the day. If you find you are more productive on a Monday morning but not a Friday afternoon then schedule important tasks when you have maximum energy levels. If you find you are more creative in the morning or late in the evening when everyone has left the office then schedule critical or creative tasks for these time periods. In the words of Benjamin Franklin,

"Lost time is never found again."

What Accounted for Most of Your Interruptions?

Let us consider that you find that Wednesday afternoon is the least productive period of the week. You identified this by looking at your daily log and found that someone keeps entering your office with questions at about 2:00 PM every Wednesday. On Friday morning, you walk into work and have to spend hours responding to email. Knowing what accounts for most of those interruptions will assist with developing steps to address them and maintain productivity.

Are you Able to Manage Your Schedule?

This is a huge influence on workplace productivity. If you find that you are constantly responding to others, you will not be able to work efficiently. You may fatigue faster and your stress levels will go up. It's much better to take control of your work schedule than to let others run your day. Plan your day to avoid long and numerous meetings consuming all your time. Try to schedule meetings throughout the day. Schedule in blocks of time in your diary just to catch up with emails, prepare for the next meeting or just some 'thinking' time to consider the next task or project.

How Can We Avoid These Distractions?

Now that you have identified why distractions occur, you are now in a position to address the distractions. If you consider pre-arranging a time for the person, to ask questions or responding to your email at another time you will be less stressed and more productive. William Penn, entrepreneur and philosopher said,

"Time is what we want most, but what we use worst."

Take a moment to review your log and look for patterns that interrupt your productivity. Then continue to use the following steps to increase workplace productivity.

Can You Use Technology to Help?

Technology can be very useful to help you manage your time. E.g. you can place your calendar on the web for your employees to see what you are doing. You can even block a section of your calendar called 'open door' which gives employees advanced notice of when they can come and see you. It is normally less time consuming to respond to an employee by email instead of talking on the phone. You will need to strike a balance, because emails are less personal than a phone call and voice tone and timber of your *communication* is omitted with an email. In some cases email could be preferable because it allows you to formalize something that was discussed earlier or attach a file or document.

Can You Delegate any Tasks?

The definition of management is to 'work through others'. If you are spending too much time working on something yourself, you will not be available to accomplish what you need to get done throughout the day. Take a moment to identify areas where a distraction could be handled by someone else. Does the interrupting person really need to take his questions to you or could he ask a coworker first? Can you have email directed to someone else and have them forward only the most important messages to you?

Can You Outsource to Someone Else?

There are certain jobs that can be done more efficiently by someone who is specialized in them. Consider payroll for example. This can be tedious, but many companies will hire a person to come by once every two weeks and do payroll for them. It saves everyone involved time because someone who is skilled in this specific task can do the work much better and faster than someone who is being distracted by other workplace issues.

Set Objective at the Start of Each Day

Mark McCormack in his book, *What they Still Don't Teach You at Harvard Business School*, writes,

"It's not life or death for me to be on time. But I take pride in knowing how long it takes to get things done. I attach the same thought and care to budgeting my personal time that I do to projecting accurate financial budgets." [21]

In your own life, you know that with smart financial planning you can make up any financial loss; however, you will never recover any time loss. Time is critical and it is the only thing that you cannot recover. You need to maximize what you achieve in the time you have. You start each day by setting achievable daily objectives. Before you leave work for the day, take a moment to make a list of each task you need to accomplish for the next day. It is better to do this at the end of your day while something is still fresh in your mind because you may forget about it by the following morning.

Follow the Objectives throughout the Day

This step is critical to maximizing workplace productivity. Take each objective and work through it until completion. Then cross it off when done. Obviously, you will need to allow for some flexibility, but this part goes hand in hand with controlling your schedule rather than letting others control your schedule.

Remember, do not open the same email twice; read and action each email after you have opened it. Do not leave emails mounting up indefinitely. If you are getting too much mail then you need to speak to the senders and reduce the number. After approximately 100 emails per day you are losing efficiency.

Did you achieve all Objectives at the End of the Day?

If you did not get everything done at the end of the day, you will need to add it to the next day's list of objectives. In addition, did anything else come up during the day that will need your attention tomorrow? If so, then add it to your daily objectives list. Use this work list to follow your objectives throughout the day.

Evaluate Your Day

What went right during the day? What did not go right? This is the part of the day where you will evaluate performance on each objective. Do not stress over what was not within your control, but pay attention and measure performance against your daily objectives. If something was not done, document why that happened. It is a good idea to take notes because then you are less inclined to forget about something. Try to identify the three biggest time wasters and develop strategies to maintain productivity that address those time wasters.

Which Areas Should You Focus On?

There are always opportunities and areas to improve. Even if things went generally well, there are always things that can be done better. Always try to strive for continuous improvement. Use down time in your day to improve on employee relationships or take time to hone your skills in new technology. Go on the web during your lunch break, if this is within your employer's policy, research any new technology or tools that may be useful to improve your productivity further.

Time for Life Long Learning

Early in the morning before your workday starts, late at night after everyone has gone home or even during your lunch break is a great time to improve yourself. You could listen to a podcast, YouTube video or read a chapter of a book. As we discussed in chapter 4, it is better to miss a meal than to miss an opportunity to improve yourself.

What Areas did you Measure and Manage?

Try and find measurable areas of your job and manage those accordingly. Find areas of your job that can be measured objectively such as number of letters typed or keeping your schedule to a half an hour per customer. The more rigid the criteria, the better it can be measured and the easier it will be to track improvements. If you focus on goals then you could establish some Key Performance Indicators (KPIs) to measure your performance. Napoleon Hill puts it well,

"Teach the students to budget and use time and above all teach the truth that time is the greatest asset available to human beings and the cheapest."

Get a Daily Planner, Filofax, or Similar Item

 Use a daily planner to stay organized. Try and schedule each objective for a certain part of the day and stick to that schedule. This will not only allow you to maintain control over schedule, but it can help facilitate communication with your employees because you can set time aside just to see them. It also helps you to measure how well you are meeting your objectives because you are measuring work against time to complete. E.g., if you only planned on taking half an hour to do a job, but it took you 45 minutes, you will need to figure out why that is. You could set an alarm on your mobile to remind you when you should finish so that you do not overrun your time. This not only allows you to stay on task, but you also get to take a five minute break to get up and stretch and go for a coffee between tasks.

Avoid Distractions

Minimizing distractions are the best way to maintain productivity at work. Turn off items like Facebook, Twitter, chat and even email. Some of these social networking sites should not be used while working if they are not a direct resource or tool required for your job. It's also best to sign out of any instant messaging clients. If you have to be on instant messaging then make sure you use an away status if you have an important task that requires completion. Turn off the cell phone or put it on silent for short periods during the day and then check your messages at designated times. Remember the purpose of being at work is to work. Stay focused on the job. Use the tools and do not let the tools use you!

Stay Productive

Following the above outlined strategies you will be able to identify areas of your work day where you can improve on productivity. Start by keeping a log of daily activities and look for patterns of where you are most productive and least productive. Identity the reasons for being less productive and develop strategies to address those reasons. Make sure that you are goal driven and setting objectives for the day. This will help you maintain control of your schedule, allowing you to be proactive rather than reactive. Delegate or outsource any tasks that can be done more efficiently by people who are specialized.

Use a day planner and minimize distractions. Take time to reflect on the day and consider where you can improve and make things better. Be sure to stay up to date with technology. Technology always provides opportunities to do things more efficiently and manage tasks better. Read books on personal growth and development and implement the suggestions into your workday. Follow these steps and you will be able to maximize your workday and be much more productive.

X Factors

- Identify where you are most productive and where you are least productive
- Complete the critical or creative task in the part of the day where you are most productive
- Set daily objectives and task lists to focus on delivering value added activities
- Set a time each day for Life Long Learning
- New Technology is good but use the tools wisely and don't let the tools use you

Chapter 6

Leadership Style

"It is better to lead from behind and to put others in front, especially when you celebrate victory when nice things occur. You take the front line when there is danger. Then people will appreciate your leadership."

\- Nelson Mandela

Introduction

We all influence people in many different ways. This is a natural part of life. The influence may be within your immediate family, social circle or may extend to church, work or other social networks you may have. Your influence could be within one town, city, country, region or even globally. Your influence could be faculty, department, business unit, small company or large corporation. John Maxwell in his book *The 21 Irrefutable Laws of Leadership* describes leadership as,

"Influence, nothing more, nothing less." [16]

Harvard Manage Mentor study materials describe the changing requirements for managers to become leaders,

"Management skills are essential. But in response to an ever-changing economic and social marketplace, managers are increasingly being called upon to be leaders as well. As a result, the ability to lead — that is, identify a vision, align people to it and motivate them to achieve it — has become even more critical for today's managers." [22]

The Difference between a Manager and a Leader

The difference between a leader and a manager is that a leader generates positive change in an organization or social group. Have you ever been in a group and one person suggests that everyone start a new activity, task or challenge? This is usually the leader in a group. If the leader did not come up with the initial suggestion then normally the leader will take the idea, build a group and push through the change. It is hard to do but with increasing your influence it becomes easier.

Paul Hoang, in his book *Business and Management* puts it like this,

"A leader is a person who influences and inspires others to get things done. An effective leader will promote loyalty, motivation, respect and trust from the workforce. Leadership is the process of influencing and inspiring others to achieve, from completing a task to achieving corporate objectives." [23]

In a work environment, leadership is easier due to the organizational structure in place; the manager's job role, title and position in the organization are clearly defined. Poor managers will exercise their title or position in the organization to get things done and drive change. This *Title* or *Positional* based leadership is the lowest form of leadership. You only follow these leaders because you have to. They may threaten you with loss of privileges, loss of bonuses, benefits or in some extreme cases loss of your job. Good leaders and managers use their personal influence to build, develop and drive teams. They very rarely have to say they are the manager or leader, they do not need to. Everyone knows that they are the natural leader and people will follow them because they know the task will get completed, on time, on budget and to an acceptable standard.

Pure Leadership

Leadership in its purest form can only be found in voluntary organizations or social situations. You find leaders in companies and large corporations however, there is the company structure, hidden rules and human resource departments to ensure that everyone is aligned and behaves in a proper and respectful manner. In a social situation with a group of friends or with colleagues after work, this is the place where you find the true leaders. Have you ever tried to organize a group of volunteers? None of them need to be available to give their time and talents to the task. None of them are contracted to arrive on time or stay until the end. None of them need to give the correct level of effort to meet the deadline or achieving the correct level of quality. How do you manage a dysfunctional array of volunteers? It could be like herding cats, they all go in their own direction! They are all there voluntarily and this is where your leadership skills are truly tested. A leader that relies solely on positional leadership at his place of employment will fail in this situation. You cannot order, coax or cajole others

to do what you want. (See illustration) You need to develop relation-ships and influence each person individually. You need to make small emotional deposits into the influence *savings bank* with each person. In some people the Influence savings bank is large with deposits and you have great influence, in others where they are new to the group then you need to start from ground zero and develop your leadership influence with them and deposit into their *savings bank*. Not everyone will be on the same level; you cannot influence everyone simultane-ously, rather, you have to build your influence slowly and deliberately over many days, weeks, months and years.

Improving Your Leadership Style

In order to improve your leadership ability join a voluntary orga-nization, charity, church, local club or social group. Meet with them as a group then work with each one individually or within a smaller group to build your influence. When you think you are ready and the *Influence Savings Banks* have enough deposits then test out your leadership abilities. Ask the group to start a new task, plan a new initiative or just try and get as many as you can to a social event like ten pin bowling, go-karting or the cinema. Practice your influencing skills by working with the most influential people in the group. Build a coalition that you are aligned with, associate with key members of the group and then one by one convincing the volunteers that they should go with your proposal. – *'we can all meet on Friday evening at 7:30pm at the cinema'*. Assess how many you invited, how many attended, for those that did not attend, what was their excuse for non attendance. Remember this is a voluntary organization, if only one or two attend the event then you have made a good start. You can build on that and maybe the next time three or four will attend.

Leadership in the Workplace

The pure leadership skills you learn in the voluntary organization will be invaluable in your workplace. In modern and global companies you are increasingly being asked to work in virtual teams. Less people are reporting directly to managers, organizational structures are flat and we are not in the same physical location. The organizational structure is more like a 'matrix' organization where most have dotted lines to someone else. The old hierarchy organization is disappearing. The modern leader needs to learn to manage and lead people that do not work for them. The modern leader has to influence people in another city or country who they have never met before. Paul Hoang defines it like this,

"An official leader, also known as a formal leader, is established by an organization and therefore has the authority to give orders to other people within the organization. An informal leader is not in an official role but has natural flair or charisma in influencing other people. Hence all leaders have the 'power' to influence, although the source of power is different for official and unofficial leaders." [23]

If you are just starting your career or new to a company it is highly likely that you will not have a team or direct reports. You need to rely on the 'power' of an unofficial leader.

Influential Leadership

You will increasingly find that you have to rely on people in other areas of the business where you have no hierarchical influence. You need to exercise all of the influencing techniques that you have learned in the voluntary organization to leverage these people and convince them that your project or task is the most important in their current task list for  that day. You are relying on them to complete the task with the correct level of time and quality in order for you to complete the larger project. Ask yourself, who would you listen to, the senior manager in the office next to you or the young high achiever in an office far away living in a country that you can't even pronounce, let alone spell? The young Generation Y'er has a much tougher job however by depositing in the *Influence Savings Bank* the Generation Y'er can start to slowly exert influence over their colleagues in a distant city and office. Please do not see influence with a negative connotation, we all need to work as a team, no man is an island. We all have different skills and we help each other to fulfill the long-term strategies and vision for our companies. As a young Generation Y'er in a new role or company you have no direct reports. There are two ways to look at this situation. You can decide that no-one works for you and you are on your own, you cannot delegate and you need to do your time until you get some direct reports or you can decide that everyone in the company works for you. You influence others in your department, office or further afield and leverage these resources to get your task or projects accomplished. Do not worry, many people are poor at this, if you are just a little better than the next person you will make a big difference and your manager will also notice.

"If you always approach everyone with cheerful optimism you'll find that they simply have no choice but to respond in kind." [20]

Your manager will notice that you build rapport quickly with people, either in person, on the phone or just by a short SMS to someone who is attending a hospital appointment, enquiring about their new baby or congratulating them on their recent wedding engagement. Rapport and influence can be built in so many ways however it has to be genuine. If you are trying to exert influence on people and have a hidden agenda or are not genuine then your colleagues will notice this, you will start to withdraw deposits from the *Influence Savings Bank* and go into the red!

Lead Yourself First

Think of this example, you now have your first assignment however, you need some assistance from a couple of colleagues in your company. One works in your office and the other works in an office in another country or across town. Before you can lead others you need to be able to lead yourself. You know and understand your strengths in Chapter 1, you know your goals and objectives in Chapter 3 and now you understand how to manage your time in Chapter 5. If you have not read these chapters then be sure to read them later.

Now that you understand your strengths it is important to understand what kind of leader you are. For example, if you identified in Chapter 1 that your key strengths were around Harmony, Empathy, Fairness, Inclusiveness and Woo? You are more focused on people. Your leadership style may be more focused on people, their thoughts and feelings and trying to make them part of the team and included.

If your strengths were more around Achiever, Activator, Command, Focus and Responsibility, then you may be more task-focused. All strengths are useful; however, remember a strength overdone is a 'WatchOut'. If your five strengths are a mixture of both sets then you are probably a middle-of-the-road manager.

"Leadership is not simply about telling others what to do. Many seem to think this and succeed in creating resentment and hostility around them. In order to understand the true qualities of a leader, the desired outcomes of leadership and to make sense of the different contexts in which leadership can be exercised, we need to first look at management generally." [24]

The best way to illustrate this point is the Blake Mouton Managerial Grid. [25] This grid describes the balance between a people-oriented approach to leadership and a task and a productive approach to leadership.

The Blake Mouton Grid of Leadership Styles

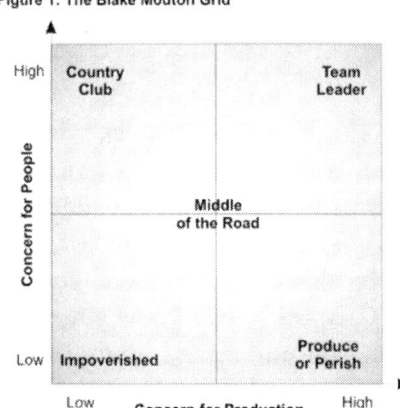

Figure 1: The Blake Mouton Grid

Along the horizontal axis we have the focus on 'Concern for Production.' This is the degree to which the leader is concerned about delivering the results, achieving the goal and meeting the objectives.

The vertical axis is focused on 'Concern for People'; this is the degree to which the leader is concerned for the people, the team, the well being of the team and their personal interests.

The five leadership styles can be identified from the chart. As you read each Leadership style try and identify your predominant style.

Impoverished Leader

This manager has very low regard for individuals and his team; he has no concern for their personal well-being, future, happiness, family or career. He also has a low regard for the task or objective that he and the team have to accomplish as part of their role within the company. He is a poor leader of people and poor contributor to the company's goals and objectives.

Produce or Perish Leader

This is the manager that is very highly task orientated. He sees the goal or objective; he eyes the prize and has no regard or concern for his team members or the team as a whole. He will 'take the hill' and complete the task even if some of his team are sick, disillusioned or leave the organization.

Country Club Leader

This is the manager that has a high concern for his team. He is concerned about each individual, their personal happiness and inclusion in the team. He wants harmony in the team and wants everyone to enjoy themselves and be happy. The manager also wants

to be liked and will go above and beyond for his team's happiness. While some of these qualities can be good in a manager we find that due to the low 'Concern for Production,' company objectives and due dates are not met. The manager may be loved by his team however the senior managers can't rely on him and his team to complete a task on time, on budget and with the correct level of quality.

Team Leader

This is the manager who has both key qualities, is a high achiever, has high focus and wants to complete the task on time and on budget; however, he is also concerned for his team and doesn't want to lose morale getting the team to the finish post. He will care for his team and keep them together making them accountable to each other. As a leader this is the best quadrant to be in. The task is completed and no one *died* in the process.

Middle of the Road Leader

This is the leader that is a bit of both. He will try and achieve the objectives however if the team are over worked or there is a problem then the goal or objective can be compromised. The manager wants to be liked by his team and ensure their personal needs are met however tasks aren't always completed on time and the team are not always considered. Sitting on the fence or in the middle of the road is not always the best place to be. You are not one thing or another but a mediocre leader at best.

Which Type of Leader are You?

It is important to identify what kind of leader you are. In practice there is no correct style however you don't want to ever be in the

'Impoverished' quadrant. Richard Templar in his book, *The Rules of Management*, puts it like this,

"Adapting your style does not mean you have to be a chameleon. It means you have to be sensitive to your team's individuality and work with it." [20]

You exercise different styles depending on the situation you are faced with. If you have no direct reports and you are trying to exercise influence over others that do not report to you then you may switch to more of a 'Country Club' leadership style. You want to influence your virtual staff members or matrix reports by being friendlier, inclusive and having a high concern for their personal needs. If you find yourself in a critical situation like an IT system has had a catastrophic failure or a machine or engineering construction has failed then you may need to switch more to a 'Produce or Perish' leadership style. This style would be more common in the military services than in a corporation; however, it can be used effectively when there is a big problem affecting the health and safety of individuals, a major event affecting your company or force majeure. You can switch to these styles for short periods until the emergency is averted and then switch more to the 'Team Leader' role when the emergency has passed. In many cases where the company is faced with a major event or catastrophe then the team members will look to their leader to take responsibility, show leadership, switch to the 'Produce or Perish' style and take the team through the problem in a constructive and systematic way. Your team will expect you to switch to this style and if you do not switch then this will damage your reputation and your 'brand'.

Switching Leadership Styles

Leadership style isn't just a function of personality. The best leaders actively choose their leadership style to fit a given situation.

"Perhaps one of the most important responsibilities of today's leaders is creating the conditions that enable employees to excel. To achieve this aim, the most successful leaders are also the most flexible: they have learned to adapt their leadership style to the situation." [22]

While some styles may be more comfortable for you to adopt than others, the more you stretch yourself to learn a range of styles, the more effective you will be as a leader. Generally speaking, being able to switch from 'Team Leader' to 'Country Club' to 'Produce or Perish' styles can maximize your team's performance and ability to deliver on company goals and objectives.

When leading people in a one-on-one situation, the style you adopt should reflect the needs and personality of the individual you are working with. It is important to remember that everyone has different capabilities and strengths which will likely fluctuate on a project-by-project basis. Therefore, the same person may need you to provide a different leadership style, depending on the task at hand. Always be flexible to switch your style when the situation or task warrants you to adopt a different approach.

X Factors

- Recognize the Difference between a Manager and a Leader
- Aim for Pure Leadership, join a charity or voluntary organization
- Remember the 5 Different Styles of a Leader
- Identify Your preferred Leadership Style
- Change Your Leadership Style when required

Chapter 7

Driving Change

"The Stone Age didn't end because people ran out of stones! It ended because people kept learning and improving."

– John Maxwell

Introduction

Change is the law of nature. Life has been changing for 1000s of years and there is no sign of it slowing down. On the contrary, in some industries change is accelerating. Rapid change used to be the bastion of high technology industries; however, even in the more traditional industrially sectors like glass, steel, rubber and tire production we are experiencing rapid change. In my early days in management in the glass and  steel industry, we experienced customer demand for increasingly new and efficient designs of ceramics. Recently in the tire industry, the customer is searching for the latest versions of tire designs. The companies that do not have an innovative design and change process both to the external customer and within their own internal organizations, will not survive long in this increasingly competitive marketplace.

Companies must constantly adapt and evolve to the different markets and customers within those markets. They must embrace new technologies, procedures, policies and processes in order to stay one-step ahead of their competitors and offer increased added value to their customers. The companies that consistently serve their customers the best will survive. Customers are becoming more and more demanding. They require smaller, faster and cheaper products and companies must increasingly embrace new technology to reduce the time to market of new designs, reduce lead-time from raw material to finished goods, increased levels of service while reducing their working capital and operating costs, improving margins and returning value back to their shareholders. With this increasing and often conflicting change, it is the responsibility of the middle managers to execute the overall vision and mission of the senior executives.

As young leaders and managers it is your responsibility to Drive change, Control change or Adapt to change within your organizations, for the very life of our organization depends on this ability to change.

"Thirty years of research by leadership guru Dr. John Kotter has proven that 70% of all major change efforts in organizations fail. Why do they fail? Because organizations often do not take the holistic approach required to see the change through." [26]

As we already discussed in the previous chapter, leaders drive change. This is what sets them apart from the managers, department heads and other employees. Here in this chapter, we will discuss how this change can happen and how we can ensure that the change process does not fail in your organizations.

Defining Change Management

Margaret Rouse, Editorial Director of whatis.com defines change management,

"Change management is a systematic approach to dealing with change, both from the perspective of an organization and on the individual level." … "For an organization, change management means defining and implementing procedures and/or technologies to deal with changes in the business environment and to profit from changing opportunities." [27]

Change management in its simplest form is Driving Change, Controlling Change and Adapting to Change.

Now that we have defined change we need to be clear and concise about the process to execute the change in our team, department or business unit.

John P. Kotter's 8 Steps to Successful Change

John P. Kotter, Harvard Business School professor and leading thinker and author on organizational change management, summarizes the change process into 8 manageable steps. Here is an overview of his 8-step process:

Step 1 - Create a sense of urgency

This first step is the most challenging. We usually underestimate what is required to overcome the stagnation of complacency in the organization to start making a change. Many are happy with the status quo and do not want you to 'rock the boat.' There is usually more than enough work to do and it is difficult enough just surviving and making it through the day without taking on yet another initiative, task or project.

Developing a sense of urgency is critical to get the project or initiative moving and gain the needed traction and cooperation. You need to inspire people to move, you need to paint the picture of the new world, the new vision or how things will be much better, make the goal real and make it relevant for them and for the organization. As a young team leader or manager, your responsibility will be to create a sense of urgency. Your people cannot see the *train coming down the track* or the *tornado about to hit the company*. The urgency can be created by taking an existing target or Key Performance Indicator (KPI) and making it almost unreachable. This will often create the urgency required to make radical change. The KPI must be firmly linked to the overall company strategy or mission; otherwise, your team will think you are crazy. If customers, suppliers or shareholders are affected by the complacency then an unhappy customer is a great way to overcome complacency within the company and start the momentum. If your change initiative touches a 'back office' department, who do not normally engage with customers, a customer visit will generate the desired level of accountability and develop a sense of urgency. The customer is now no longer some remote and mystical entity but a real person and organization that will benefit from your change initiative.

Make the team responsible and accountable to each other and you can start to create momentum. Large companies are like *massive oil tankers with very small rudders*. It is very difficult to turn them and move in a different direction. John Maxwell sums it up well,

"If you've got all the passion, tools and people you need to fulfill a great vision, yet you can't seem to get your organization moving and going in the right direction, you're dead in the water as a leader." [28]

Create the urgency to make a start in your change initiative.

Step 2 - Build the guiding team

Any change requires strong leadership. The size and level of the guiding team depends on the size of the change. If the change is only affecting a small team or department then the team leader or manager should identify the key stakeholders and start to work with them, build personal relationships and leverage these resources to help drive through the change. If the change affects the whole company then you need to garner support from the top level CEO, his direct reports and other senior executives. Change should be driven from the top, or where the change starts and must be owned and adopted by the bottom in order to be successful.

The team leader or manager should also identify any *hidden leaders* within the organization to be changed. The hidden leaders are people within the organization that may not have a senior title or high position; however, they are highly respected in the organization, people turn to them for leadership and guidance and they can influence and sway opinion. They often have a large support base and they are a valuable addition to your guiding team. If these hidden leaders agree to the change then your job will be much easier and they will assist you. If you do not win the hearts and minds of these individuals then the change effort will be an uphill struggle, it could stall and fail. Get the right people in the right place with the right commitment. Ensure they have the right mix of management and leadership skills and are at the correct level of the organization to push through a change.

If the change just touches a small team, department or business unit then middle managers and leaders will be good enough to drive the change. Choose your guiding team carefully. They can be a formal team, sponsor group or committee; alternatively, it can be an unofficial team if the change is small. Include various stakeholders that will be accountable for the successful change. John Maxwell says,

"People buy into the leader first and then the vision." [28]

Ensure you select leaders and managers of good standing and a good reputation in order to drive through the change. This leadership and management selection is a crucial step. Remember the best leader may not necessarily be the most senior person in terms of age, title or position in the organization. Look for the hidden leaders in the organization. This may surprise you but some of the best hidden leaders are works council or union officials! Try to leverage these leaders in your change initiative.

Step 3 - Get the vision right

In a large corporation the senior executives will normally set a clear vision and mission that may be used internally to drive the direction of the business and also shared with external stakeholders like customers, suppliers, shareholders and trade bodies. The vision and mission should convey a picture of a new world, describe what the future will look like and make it desirable for the organization to go in that direction. The vision should be realistic and achievable in a reasonable timescale. It should be clear, focused and should be easy to communicate in various forms to the whole organization.

Examples;

For the US in 1961 the mission was, "landing a man on the moon and returning him safely to the earth, by the end of the decade." [29]

For a global corporation the mission is,

"All around the world, Goodyear's purpose is to increase the value of our brands for everyone. With market-driven innovation, delivering the highest quality tires, related products and services for our customers and consumers." [30]

For a department a mission statement could be,

"Reduce Accounts Receivables from 120 days to 30 days by end of the year."

"Improve on time delivery by 9% by August."

If the change only affects a small team or department then the process of creating a vision is similar. Initially, as discussed earlier, it should align to the corporate vision and mission statement. The vision or mission will more than likely take the form of a department goals or objectives. It should be clear and concise like the corporate vision and should align to SMART principals, Specific, Measureable, Achievable, Realistic and Time bound. You also need to communicate the vision to the entire team in an easy way. Sometimes it helps to draw the vision in the form of a chart, graph, KPI or picture in order to focus the team's attention.

If you are new in your management or leadership role then practice introducing small changes within your area of influence and control first. Then build your confidence with defining a goal or objective and driving change. Over time, you can increase the size of the change until you become more confident in your use of the 8-step change process.

Step 4 - Communicate for buy-in

For the team leader, department head or middle manager trying to drive a change, it is important for you to design and develop a clear vision and communicate it in such a way so that your communication does not drown in the sea of communication that your company transmits to its employees on a regular basis. You need to 'brand' your change initiative in such a way that it is seen, understood and internalized to those that you want to change. Kotter writes,

"The real power of a vision is unleashed only when most of those involved in an enterprise or activity have a common understanding of its goals and direction. That shared sense of a desirable future can help motivate and coordinate the kinds of actions that create transformations." [31]

Keep your change vision simple. Use simple words to <u>describe</u> your change initiative. Use a metaphor, example or picture to <u>present</u> your vision. Use numbers or KPIs to <u>define</u> your change initiative. Good communication appeals to all 3 learning styles; those that prefer words, pictures and numbers. First select a picture that describes your change initiative, then write a tagline or similar to describe it then make it measureable by adding a KPI or target. Your vision will then stand out from the 'sea of sameness' and the wave of other internal communication vying for people's attention.

Now that you are armed with your vision statement you should involve as many people as possible and communicate the vision using as many communication channels as possible; posters in the office, email communication, team meetings, conference calls, wallet cards and laminated sheets in the office. Use all means possible to market your change initiative. Communication must be simple, appealing and accessible in order to gain excitement for your change initiative.

I personally believe we are moving from the Information age to the Entertainment age. We have myriads of information available to us and now more and more people want to be 'entertained' by that information. Sending a bland email out to employees is not going to cut it anymore. The email must be bright and colorful and appealing if you want your message to have an impact. In the past a simple presentation with a few words was seen as state of the art over the old transparency projectors some of us used. Now presentations need to be colorful, entertaining and appealing to the modern viewer who has much less time to absorb information and gets bored easily. If your communications are not short and snappy then the demands of emails, calls and messaging will steal the attention of your audience. Make your vision presentations fit to one A4 piece of paper or one presentation slide. If you require more than this then your vision is too complicated and it cannot be communicated to your team easily and effectively.

"If you can't explain it simply, you don't understand it well enough."
- Albert Einstein

Step 5 - Empower action

Now that you have your change vision and you have communicated it to the team you now need to execute the vision. In order for a change initiative to be successful it requires everyone's involvement, i.e. all the stakeholders in the process or at least the major ones. People need to feel that they are empowered to get behind the vision and the change initiative and that they can make the difference. In order to empower the employees it is important to remove as many of the barriers to change as possible. Some barriers may include the organizational structure, the current reporting lines and staffing. Responsibilities may not align to the new way of working; some supervisors or other team leaders may oppose the change and therefore this should be addressed. Employees will need training in the new process, system, or procedure you want to introduce. Some people are fearful of the unknown; others enjoy uncertainty and find it exciting. Train the staff to the correct level that they fully understand the new change being introduced, they can ask questions, there is 2-way dialogue and they are at ease with the change. Win each person to the side of change, one person, one team and one department at a time. Empower each of them to drive through the change. Supervisors, team leaders and managers need to demonstrate the change and they need to vocally support the change in order to influence their teams. If the management structure does not support the change nor do they feel empowered then this will need to be addressed. Naysayers can be toxic to a change initiative and need to be realigned or removed from the process.

Step 6 - Create short-term wins

The big dream or vision is important but remember to split this into short-term wins also. Plan short-term wins into your change process. People sometimes get weary with a long-term change initiative and therefore need a short-term win to encourage them to go further and commit more and work longer hours if necessary. Employees need to see the plan working and the vision being realized. This will give them the renewed energy and excitement to continue.

Set short-term objectives that can be attained easily and then celebrate the success. Finish current stages before starting new ones. This will give you a sense of satisfaction on achieving the goals.

Communicate the win to the team, department and to your manager. Ensure everyone knows that your change initiative is working and achieving the desired results. If you do not have short-term wins then the team will become weary and the change initiative will fizzle out, regress and die.

Step 7 - Don't give up

Now that you have the short-term wins it now becomes important to recognize this. Celebrate and recognize those individuals and departments who were involved with the change; however, do not over celebrate. Kotter describes in his book instances where companies have over celebrated a short-term win and the company sinks into the sea of complacency. They pat themselves on the back for their success and then return to their old ways. The change effort slows because the employees think they have arrived and the change process is completed. You need to maintain the momentum for the change effort. You need to celebrate the change while also fostering and encouraging determination and persistence to keep going and achieve the future milestones of the department, business unit and organization. Keep pushing........

Step 8 - Make change stick

Reinforce the value of the successful change. Weave the change into the culture of the organization so that it becomes easy for staff to accept the changes for a better tomorrow. This may include building the change into the company's core values and updating policies and procedures. The change should also be clearly defined into the job descriptions of the employees throughout the team, department or organization.

Annual objectives and targets should also be aligned to the change. In large change projects it may be necessary to change the organizational reporting structure to align to the change. In extreme cases those that oppose the change  may be removed and new individuals brought into the team or department who will support and maintain the change and enshrine into the culture of the organization.

The change needs to form the new DNA for the company. The change should be entrenched, absorbed and internalized by all individuals. If only one person adopts the change then the departure of this person will cause the whole change effort to slowly deteriorate, regress and collapse. This last step is the most important in the change process. I picture it like rolling a large rock up a hill. If you do not place a block under the rock then it will roll down on top of you. Move the rock up the hill slowly and deliberately and place the block under at suitable times to avoid disaster.

Laying the Foundation for Change

Some employees may be resistant to the changes. Try to identify them early in the change process, understand their motives and then apply techniques to assist with their difficulties. Sometimes the introduction of the new technology or software can be frightening to some people. Find out what motivates them, meet them one-on-one and try to find solutions to assist them with the change process. Every person is different; we all absorb change at different speeds. If you notice that some individuals are struggling with the change then meet them individually. If there are departments, teams, or large groups that have not grasped the change then cast the vision to them again, communicate to them in different ways. Email, newsletters, company bulletin boards, online video and meetings all serve to communicate the same message but in different ways.

Organizing social gatherings and interactive sessions will also aid to the process of change, this will bring members of the organization closer and informal discussion may arise which can effectively clear any doubt and convince peers that change is better. We have talked about the different processes, which can be initiated to achieve the desired goal of change in the organization or individual. Now, we will discuss how this process of change management can be helpful in identifying the potential change managers and leaders needed for the expansion of our business.

How to Emerge as Leader of Positive Change

Be innovative, deliver more than what is expected from you, be proactive to get noticed and present your ideas when asked or when you find the opportune moment. Focus on the *solution in the problem and not the problem in the solution*. Appreciate the work of colleagues and assist them when they are in trouble or difficulty, we are all one team. We win as a team or lose as a team. The change we wish to see will be possible only when we build our network to be ready for the time that we want to drive through a change.

Your level of influence is different with every person. The level of change will determine the level of influence you need to exert on the different members of the organization. If you are senior in an organization then your position will assist you to drive through change. If you are lower in the organization or you are in a voluntary organization then you will need to use all these X factors to assist you. Develop a personal and genuine concern for each member of the organization and you will develop into a great driver, controller and adapter of change. John Maxwell puts it well,

"Leaders touch a heart before they ask for a hand." [28]

Change Requires a High Level of EQ

Everyone absorbs change at a different pace. Use your EQ and understand how others are feeling about the change being implemented. Are they OK with the change? Do they have technical, process, or organizational reasons why the change cannot take place or do they just have a fear of the unknown? If some employees start to have regular absence or periods of sickness then this could be an early sign that they are not coping well with the change in the department or organization. On one occasion, I had an experience of an employee who had never been sick for many years, suddenly have periods of sickness. After further discussion with the individual, I identified that he was not happy with a new computer system that had been introduced. It is crucial to use your EQ and identify small and subtle changes in the behavior of your team during the change process. As I said at the beginning of the chapter, change is constant therefore as young managers and leaders you should be aware of any subtle changes in behavior of your direct reports or working colleagues. This will show the early stages of stress, much of which is a result of change.

Leaders Drive the Change

Change management can be a productive and innovative method of improving the performance of our organizations. This chapter has discussed and presented that a structured approach to change management will ensure that change initiatives are successful and embedded into the DNA of the organization. The active participation of the team leader or middle manager is key to any change within your organization and you have a responsibility to ensure that you Drive, Control and Adapt to any change management initiative.

The difference between a manager and a leader is that leaders drive change in an organization where a manager maintains current and established processes and procedures. If you want to be a leader, you need to practice and hone your skills in the change management process.

X Factors

- Align the change process to the company's overall Vision and Mission
- Understand Kotter's 8 step change process
- For each change identify if you are a Driver, Controller or Adapter of the change
- Be open to change in your personal and professional life
- Use your EQ to identify how your colleagues and direct reports are managing with change (more in Chapter 8)

Chapter 8

Developing Your Emotional Intelligence (EQ)

"Emotional intelligence emerges as a much stronger predictor of who will be most successful"
- Daniel Jay Goleman

Introduction

In this chapter we will discuss the primary X-Factor that will influence your long-term personal and career success. Emotional intelligence (EQ) is defined as being able to evaluate and control one's own emotions, as well as to understand and react in a suitable manner to the emotions of others. In the corporate world, we are faced with ever increasing challenges that require a great deal of emotional effort to both understand our own emotions in a particular situation and also understand the emotions of our work colleagues, peers, managers and also our internal and external customers.

Today's work environment can be very stressful with increasingly short deadlines and a reduction in human and financial resources. Understanding how you feel about these challenges will increase your ability to cope in these situations and handle periods of stress, fear and anxiety. It is important to be able to identify your own emotions quickly and be able to control your emotions in a suitable way in order to manage your engagement and interaction with others. When professionals openly express emotions and lack control, they can be perceived as being weak, unstable and lacking in consistency. In the *Emotional Intelligence 2.0* book, Bradberry and Greaves write,

"Your EQ is the foundation for a host of critical skills – it impacts most everything you say and do each day. EQ is so critical to success that it accounts for 58 percent performance in all types of jobs. It's the single biggest predictor of performance in the workplace and the strongest driver of leadership and personal excellence …… Of all the people we've studied at work, we have found that 90 percent of high performers are also high in EQ." [32]

If you find that your EQ is particularly low you will find that it is harder for peers, direct reports and managers to work with you and learn how to best interact with you. Being able to control your emotions will keep you from uncontrolled outbursts during high stress situations and saying something you regret and damaging the long term working relationship. Likewise, being able to assess other people's emotions is equally as important so that you understand how to work with them. Daniel Jay Goleman, an author, psychologist and science journalist writes,

"If your emotional abilities aren't in hand, if you don't have self-awareness, if you are not able to manage your distressing emotions, if you can't have empathy and have effective relationships, then no matter how smart you are, you are not going to get very far." [33]

Furthermore, one of the biggest communication flaws in the corporate world is not being able to adjust one's communication strategy to different people and emotional states. Possessing the ability to do this will allow you to better understand other people in their time of weakness, ultimately making yourself a better communicator and more successful manager and leader in the workplace. You should not confuse IQ (Intelligence Quotient) with EQ (Emotional Quotient), IQ is a measure of your intellect, capacity and capability to solve complex challenges and problems while EQ is a measure of how you manage and control your own emotions and also understand and build relationships with others. Daniel Jay Goleman writes,

"There is zero correlation between IQ and emotional empathy… They're controlled by different parts of the brain." [33]

Some of the most intelligent people you will work with have a very poor understanding of their emotions and very poor social skills when interacting with others. If you learn to understand and control your emotions you will have an X-Factor.

The X Factor for Generation Y

Bradberry and Greaves, describe Generation Y as those born between 1979 and 1991. The Generation Y are less likely to be able to manage and control their emotions compared to older generations, Generation X (1966-1978), Baby Boomers (1948-1965) and Traditionalists (1929-1947). They describe that although Generation Y are much more technically savvy and have a mastery over modern technology, they have much less knowledge and mastery over their own emotions. They describe that management and leadership of others will be a challenge to them. All is not lost for the Generation Y. They proved that EQ will naturally increase as you become older; however, the Generation Y'er that can grasp the EQ concepts quicker, manage their emotions and recognize the emotions in others will have a competitive edge over others. Their studies proved that EQ is the most important leadership skill you can learn. Those with the highest EQ will outperform their peers in the workplace and command much higher salaries. It is up to each Generation Y'er to accelerate their EQ learning, this is the primary X-Factor for Generation Y.

EQ in the Workplace

In the modern workplace, we interact with others around the globe in different time zones and across different cultures. In some cases you may never have met some of your work colleagues and this interaction may have been limited to a conference call or brief telephone conversation. If you work somewhere which embraces modern technologies then they may have telepresence or video conference facilities, while others utilize webcams and other technology to bridge communication gaps in an attempt to make interactions more 'human'. EQ, however, is critical in all situations. A formal video conference at one extreme to a chance meeting and discussion at the coffee machine, EQ should be employed and is foundational for all meetings whether it is face to face or with the use of modern technology. Our communications are becoming shorter and shorter and much more 'casual,' tasks are discussed, agreements made and next steps actioned based upon short SMS, instant messages or brief telephone calls. Your EQ should be used in all interactions. It is not a tool to be used at will, it should be an integral part of your character and you should be aware of it at all times. It's like breathing. We need air to survive but we are not conscious of the breathing process. If you are naturally high in EQ then it will come naturally to you; however, if you are low in EQ then it will have to be a conscious effort to understand your emotions and keep them in control.

The EQ Edge

The most competent work colleagues you will meet are both strong at understanding and controlling their emotions and are excellent relationship builders. They watch others and can adjust their approach, discussion and interaction with others in order to achieve results for themselves, their department and their company. One simple interaction could determine if business is concluded in a mutually favorable way and future encounters with that person will be favorable. It is therefore important to remember that a bad impression, through lack of EQ, may leave someone with a total misunderstanding of you as a person and cause issues when you engage with them at a later date. Business relationships will be strained and your interaction with that person the next time will be less than favorable.

With much of our social interaction now taking place via social media and other technology, we find that some people are more comfortable with virtual communication. I have observed work colleagues emailing co-workers that are located in the next office. It would be very easy for a person to simply speak with them in person and lift their head above their desk, but of course it involves less EQ to communicate with someone by email and avoid the human interaction. Some people are more comfortable with this level of communication. In a work environment, the person who understands their emotions, communicates and is able to interact with others in a pleasant and satisfactory way is the one who will excel. He or she can get things done much quicker, making vast improvements within the workplace and drive through change which is the mark of a true leader. This will be noticeable by others as well, because a person's work colleagues will see that he or she completes tasks efficiently. If you are looking for more advice to improve your EQ then let's refer to the work of Bradberry and Greaves again, they write,

"We haven't yet been able to find a job in which performance and pay aren't tied closely to EQ." [32]

So we have learned that our EQ is foundational to everything we do in the workplace, it will allow us to be successful at our job and is directly related to our job performance and salary. Enough reasons indeed to understand and improve your EQ.

Self-awareness

Being emotionally intelligent will grant you the ability to communicate with a wider range of people, which is vital in our diverse world. The first step to emotional intelligence is to get to know ourselves.

"When you are self-aware you are far more likely to pursue the right opportunities, put your strengths to work and – perhaps more importantly – keep your emotions from holding you back." [32]

If we know how we react and what our common emotions are under certain circumstances, it will be much easier for us to take control. In the workplace, it is common to have feelings such as insecurity, jealousy, anxiety or stress and anger. Self studying your own behavior and learning more about yourself will help to reduce these feelings. You may recall the expression, *"It is not _what_ you know but _who_ you know."* You must be able to understand your own strengths and weaknesses. The expression now is, *'It is not _what_ you know but _how you know yourself.'*' Understanding your own emotions, how they modify your behavior and how this can assist you in engaging with others within the workplace is vital for your long term career success. In Julia West's work on feelings she describes 8 different types of feelings; Happy, Sad, Angry, Confused, Afraid, Weak, Strong and Guilty. She also rates each feeling's level of intensity as High, Medium or Mild. [34] When you are experiencing intense emotions stop and take 5 minutes to review your emotions. What are you feeling right now? Are you feeling sad? Are you feeling afraid? If you are afraid, are you terrified or are you just nervous? Initially define one clear emotion or feeling. After more practice you may be able to identify 2 or 3 emotions or feelings that you are experiencing. It is only after you define these feelings that you can then learn to manage them. You cannot manage something that you can't define or quantify.

Remember that if you have a serious problem in managing your emotions, you can always go to a coach, mentor or accountability partner to assist you. They can ask questions to help you define your top 3 emotions. By talking, sharing and expressing your emotions to someone else this may help you in your journey to self discovery.

Self Control

Once you are more aware of your own emotions it is then import-ant to control and manage your emotions correctly. When you are Happy, Angry or Sad then you should understand when to talk, when to listen and when to take action. You can express your feelings ver-bally to others if this helps the discussion but do not show excessive and uncontrolled emotions. You should control your emotions and don't let your emotions control you. When you become emotional you may say or do something you regret. In the workplace this can be very damaging and can impede the working relationships and col-laboration with your colleagues. You must take every opportunity to understand and control your emotions and stay consistent with your feelings and engagement with others. If you can exercise self control in heated and stressful situations then your work colleagues and those that engage with you will be less likely to *push your buttons* and cause you to lose control. They will in turn respect you much more. Your work colleagues and manager may be more aware of your feelings and emotions than you are.

You need to master and control your feelings and emotions first or your peers and colleagues may do it for you!

Awareness of People

When you are talking you are not listening. When you are talking you are also not learning from others. Listen more to others, understand why they use certain words, voice tones and also look for the non-verbal clues. When you are talking to someone, it is important not to forget to analyze that person's body language, facial expression, tone of voice and position of hands, feet and other signs. If you pay attention to these details, you will be surprised as to how their body language and yours can completely change the *conversation*. Be more aware of people and put yourself in their shoes. What are they thinking now? What is their body language *saying*? During the discussion or presentation how will they react? What was the last meeting or appointment they had before you met with them? Maybe they are still considering this. What is the next meeting or appointment on their schedule? Maybe they are mentally preparing for that. Will they be open to your proposal or will they reject because the timing is not correct? Their feelings and thoughts may be contra to your proposal or is your proposal just not suitable.

Timing is critical. In a work situation you need to interact and work together for the common benefit of the company. If the timing is not correct then you should sense this and come back another day when the situation is better. Your manager or colleagues may reject a proposal, not because it is unsuitable but because you were not aware of their emotions or feelings at the time and you pitched your point in the wrong way. If you are unsure of someone's feelings then why not just ask. I have seen this done quite effectively. If the person does not feel threatened by the question or the person asking the question then they will often express what they are feeling. This can help you determine how to approach the person during the discussion and may result in a more favorable outcome.

Building Relationships

It is extremely important to properly manage our emotions otherwise the workplace can become very political and communication is difficult. This could result in conflicts that deteriorate relationships, affect the performance and lower the level of productivity within the organization.

It is commonly known that the more senior you get in an organization, the higher your emotional intelligence must be; however, the research from Bradberry and Greeves reveals that as you become senior in the organization your EQ increases until you attain the position of middle management. As you are promoted in the organization to director, executive and CEO their research shows that your EQ actually decreases. Astonishing but true. Whether you are part of a team or you manage a small team or large department your effectiveness and therefore a successful career is based primarily on your relationships with others. For sure you need to be technically competent but all things being equal a high EQ and ability to build good solid relationships throughout the organization will improve your ability to get things done and drive through change. Driving change is the primary measure of a leader.

Can EQ be Improved?

The book *Emotional Intelligence 2.0* and its associated online test will help you to measure your EQ and also improve it. At the time of writing the test was under $40 and well worth the investment. After you have taken the online test you can learn from the results and then take the test again at a later date to chart your progress. (visit www.x4gy.com).

Today we know that emotionally intelligent people are more successful in life and more effective in communicating and managing their emotions. This, however, does not mean that those who do not possess the skill of emotional intelligence will not succeed. If you spend more time working and engaging with others with a high EQ then this will 'rub off' on you. You in turn will become more EQ savvy. Identify those you work with, your peer group and manager who have a higher level of EQ and watch how they interact with people. When do they speak? When do they listen? When do they 'people watch' and what are they learning from the behaviors' of others? Find a coach or mentor that is also high in EQ and ask them for advice. They can also assist you in preparing for a meeting, presentation or other work related activity. They can help you understand your current emotions and what you are likely to expect from others during the meeting. They can assist you with good questioning, to emotionally prepare you for the encounter.

Emotional intelligence can certainly be improved throughout life as long as you make a conscious effort to improve. Like any other skill you can slowly lose it if you don't take time to practice and perfect this skill.

The First Seven Seconds

"It takes only seven seconds for us to judge another person when we first meet them," says Linda Blair, clinical psychologist and author of *Straight Talking.* [35] This in itself shows how vital it is to make a good first impression. According to Albert Mehrabian, most of a message that is absorbed by listeners is only about 7% verbal, which is the perception of words and language. 38% of a message that is understood is purely vocal, which consists of tone of voice and other sounds. Finally, the majority of a message, 55%, is understood through non-verbal cues such as facial expressions. [36] This is intriguing, as most of us are under the assumption that words are the most important aspect of communication.

It also demonstrates that our emotional brain responds more quickly to non-verbal clues and communication than our thinking brain.

There are many non-verbal behaviors that can positively or negatively influence a first impression, including dress-code, mannerisms and also eye-contact. [37] This certainly translates to real life, as the first impression is said to stick.

First impressions can also differ according to gender. For example, women have been shown to be more physically observant and when someone's body language does not agree with their verbal communication, women often pay more attention to non-verbal cues rather than what has been said. [38]

Meeting someone for the first time

There are many do's and don'ts for communication and behavioral styles when meeting someone for the first time. How you communicate non-verbally is extremely important as your behavior could easily turn someone off, or alternatively they could like you even more. The first suggestion when meeting someone new is to smile frequently. Not only will smiling work to make you less nervous (smiling can be a self-fulfilling prophecy for making yourself feel more positive), but it can also reassure the other person of your intentions, or settle them if they are nervous.

A strong handshake is also a good sign because it demonstrates that you are stable, confident and know what you want, while also showing that you have good intentions. Having a weak handshake or no handshake at all is similar to not being able to hold eye-contact with someone as it suggests that you are nervous or have something to hide.

Is EQ Dead?

With the advancement of computer and communications technology you may believe that we no longer need emotional intelligence.

We tend to spend much of our time in front of the computer engaging in tasks such as writing emails, composing documents, instant messaging and chat, while interacting with others using Facebook, Twitter and other social media websites. In today's workplace, we are presented with fewer opportunities than before to meet face-to-face with people and interact. Because of this, it is extremely critical that we fully understand EQ and why it is important, as well as how we can develop and cultivate it. EQ is far from dead. Throughout this chapter I trust that you understand that a high EQ is critical to your personal and career success and is a key X-Factor.

X Factors

- Work on your EQ. It is critical to securing a job and long term career
- Develop your self-awareness
- Work on your self control in times of stress in the workplace
- Be more aware of people when you interact with them
- Develop good solid working relationships

Chapter 9

Find a Personal Coach & Mentor

"No process in history has done more to facilitate the exchange of information, skills, wisdom and contacts than mentoring."

– Keith Ferrazzi

Introduction

Tiger Woods requires a coach, Sean Foley, to improve his golf swing. Andy Murray requires a coach, Ivan Lendl, to improve his tennis game. Jessica Ennis, British heptathlon gold medal winner in the 2012 London Olympics, was coached by Toni Minichiello. In the world of Formula One, Sebastian Vettel has a fitness coach and physiotherapist, Tommi Pärmäkoski, to keep him in peak physical condition for the grueling Formula One races. These sportsmen are at the top of their profession and understand that they require coaching to improve their skills and keep them at the top. They also recognize that friends, family and colleagues, although willing to support, can only help their career so much. Usually at the beginning of a career a father or mother can offer some good advice on training; however, if you want to reach the top of your sport you require specialist knowledge and assistance. They came to a time when they required a professional coach to improve their game and take them to the next level.

In the world of business and your career, it is no different. Advice from friends and family is not always going to be good enough to advance your career. The most expensive career advice you will receive will be free advice from friends, family and the man in the bar that you have just met!

If you are serious about your career and personal development then you should follow the example of the top sportsmen and seek out a respected and qualified coach to assist you.

George Zalucki is the author of *Network Marketing Straight Talk* and a motivational speaker. While on stage in Budapest, he made the following comment,

"I am not alone, I have had teachers, mentors, coaches, trainers and elders influence my life." [39]

You are also a product of many teachers, trainers and elders in your life. Do not leave the advantage of this reference group to random meetings, discussions with friends and family gatherings. Make a conscious effort to seek out a coach and mentor.

Coaching vs. Mentoring

To describe coaching, it is easier to begin with what it isn't. It is not, therapy, training, mentoring, counseling or teaching. It is a relatively new style of personal development that aims to help people find the answers from within. Usually the development needed is a change in deep rooted habits and behaviors based on a person's beliefs. Therefore, the coaching experience will be asking questions to reveal their solutions. The person being coached should find the answer from their own experience and knowledge.

The term of the coaching arrangement can be from a few weeks, months or up to a year. John Whitmore, describes coaching like this,

"Coaching is unlocking people's potential to maximize their own performance. It is helping them to learn rather than teach them." [40]

Mentoring is much different, the mentor provides guidance from their own experience; they are usually more senior and the one with the knowledge and experience to offer advice. This may also be a longer-term relationship between the mentor and mentee. The mentor may assist with prolonged personal, professional and psychological development to assist the mentee in their long-term personal and career aspirations. In some cases, the mentor-mentee engagement could be a lifelong agreement to meet and support the younger mentee over the length of their career.

In this chapter, I will use the term *coaching;* however, some quotations refer to *mentoring.* For the purpose of this chapter and the X-Factors we wish to explore, please consider the words as synonymous.

Keith Ferrazzi in his book, *Never Eat Alone,* states,

"I realized that finding a talented, experienced mentor who is willing to invest the time and effort to develop you as a person and a professional is far more important than making career decisions based purely on salary or prestige." [41]

Don't underestimate the value you place on coaching.

Formal Definition of Coaching

"The International Coach Federation (ICF) defines coaching as partnering with clients in a thought-provoking and creative process that inspires them to maximize their personal and professional potential. Coaching honors the client as the expert in his/her life and work and believes that every client is creative, resourceful and whole.

Coaches work with people who want support in their jobs, their projects, or their personal development. They work with individuals and with teams who are looking for the best ways to get things done. A coaching partnership offers a confidential space to explore ideas, problem-solve and establish a realistic, clear plan of action to reach desired outcomes.

The benefits of professional coaching are numerous-fresh perspectives on challenges and opportunities, enhanced thinking and decision making skills, enhanced interpersonal effectiveness and increased confidence in carrying out chosen work and life roles." [42]

Who needs a Coach?

At some point in your job or career, you will reach a time when you have a particular challenge. You may require a new technical skill, presentation advice, or management guidance to assist you. This may be because you have been given a new task or assignment that requires new skills or it could be that you have been recently promoted to a new position and are a bit overwhelmed with the new job role and responsibilities.

Seeking out, finding and asking someone to help you is not a sign of weakness; it should be seen as a positive indication that you require a particular skill and are willing to learn and invest in your career. A simple example could be presentation skills. You have been asked to prepare a presentation for new clients and you are unsure about the use of software or how to build the presentation, how you should format your message and then how to deliver this message to the new clients. You may seek out someone in your organization known for creating excellent presentations; you seek out *The Presentations Person.* This is the person in the organization who has established the reputation and 'branding' of developing excellent presentations. If you approach *The Presentations Person,* most of the time they will be glad to share their knowledge. Although a coach will not help you with the presentation they will help you explore possibilities to find further help or discover other options available to you.

In the words of Lord Sebastian Coe, Olympic runner, "Find out what you don't know then find someone who knows and ask them to help you."

If you have been recently promoted to a senior position within your organization. You may require broader skills in your mindset and behaviors while managing people, setting personal objectives and ongoing development of yourself and your staff. In this example, you may look for a more senior and mature manager who has these skills. This may be someone you respect in the organization for being a good people person and managing his team well or it may be someone in your social circle that you admire such as someone in your special interest group, sports teams, or local church. If you cannot find a suitable person then search online and there will be professional coaches in your area that may be able to assist you.

Coaches are all around you. Firstly identify the skill or task you require assistance with, then keep your eyes open and identify someone that you admire who demonstrates these skills. If you are really stuck then contact a careers advisor, recruitment consultant, or your Human Resources department; they can assist you to search out a coach in a particular area. One word of advice, if you require a particular skill, do not automatically seek out the latest and greatest training course and request to attend the next available one. Many times, we need specific skills to help us get over the next challenge; you need a mix of learning such as experiential learning and coaching. In the experiential learning you learn and stretch yourself by trying a new task, a job switch, or rotation with a peer. You accept a new short-term project or initiative or volunteer for a new task. A formal training course may provide you with a nice shiny certificate to put on your office wall but may be of little use to help you learn a specific skill or take on your next management challenge.

A great way to improve your leadership skills is to join a local volunteer group or charity. Volunteering not only allows you to give something back to the community but can also be very rewarding to practice and improve your leadership ability. You could volunteer to work in a local charity, sports team, special interest group, or local church. This can accelerate your training in management and leadership because pure leadership only happens in voluntary organizations. The volunteers are not required to attend and therefore your management techniques can be fine-tuned and honed in this context to ensure that you are considerate to others and consider everyone's point of view. It is not compulsory for anyone to join a volunteer organization. The clue is in the name and therefore you need to be particularly aware of your interaction and EQ when dealing with these people. In a corporate, work organization, people are paid to give their time and skills to the organization; however, in a voluntary organization the people give their time freely due to a motivation to help people and give something back to the community. This will stretch and grow your leadership skills of connecting, respect, influence, empowerment, building momentum for change, sacrifice, timing and building a legacy.

Remember, coaching is only one form of education. Consider also experiential training and then finally, if your particular requirements are acute or are new to your field of expertise, seek out a suitable training course.

Assistance with your Long-Term Vision

A good coach can assist you to define your vision in life through analysis of your primary passion, key interests and strengths. They will guide you through a number of direct and searching questions to examine yourself and identify these high-level vision and goals. The coach just acts like a mirror to reflect your ideas back to you and challenge your thinking. If you want to know the meaning of life or why you are on this planet then I would suggest you talk to a church leader for these types of questions. There are coaching companies that may be able to offer guidance in this area however; it is not in the scope of this chapter to discuss spiritual coaching.

Assistance with Goal Setting

If you are struggling with long-term goal setting then a coach can assist you with this also. After defining your life vision, they can assist you with short, medium and long-term goal setting. Remember the coach will not give you the answers they will only ask you the questions to understand your reality and draw the answers from you. In the words of Tony Stoltzfus,

"[The coach will] make people think about something important, draw out a person's identity or touch their deepest desires." [43]

Be prepared to be asked some tough questions. It is not a test where you pass or fail. Some of these questions you will never have been asked before. They will make you stop and think and reconsider

your life. What would you like to do in 5 years time? What is stopping you doing that tomorrow? What skills do you need to get there? Each day are you completing tasks and activities that will take you closer to your long-term goal or further away from your goal?

Effective Planning & Accountability

A coach can assist you with the planning process to reach your desired goals or end state. They could propose online materials or other educational resources to help you in your journey. Sometimes the person is not aware that some materials exist. A professional coach is immersed in these materials and is aware how to find them and use them correctly. They can advise the best practice to assist you. A coach can also be an accountability partner for you. If you set goals and objectives then they can hold you accountable to ensure the goals follow the SMART principals and that you keep to the dates you committed and agreed to. An accountability partner is a very powerful addition in your life-long learning and development process. Accountability partners can come from many areas. It could be a friend. You make a commitment to him/her to complete something on time. It could be someone in another company that is keeping you accountable to completing an assignment or piece of work. The assignments and dates are always yours. It is not the responsibility of the coach to set you assignments and set dates when you will complete them, this is your job. The coach will just ensure you keep to your own promises and commitments. The work is on your side, e.g. I have an accountability partner, Lori, who is based in Canada. I have never met her or seen a picture and I could walk past her in the street and not know who she is. We have talked 2-3 times by phone and some emails. I have no contractual obligations to her whatsoever. Lori ensures I keep to my commitments to deliver what I agreed to. She will not get angry or upset if I do not deliver but she is my accountability partner and I feel an obligation to her to fulfill my promises to myself. A good accountability partner will push you higher and further than you would normally drive yourself. Your growth happens when you step out of your current box and way of thinking; your accountability partner can help you get there.

The magic happens when you get out of your box!

Developing Habits for Ongoing Success

Your coach will meet you periodically to review your progress. This may be once per month or once per quarter depending on what has been mutually agreed. The coach will check that you are continuing on your path of life-long learning and development and check that you have not slipped back. If you were given tasks or actions to complete before the next meeting then by setting regular meeting times you will be sure to stay on task and complete the assignment you mutually agreed. They will call out things you have done or not completed to keep you focused.

Explore Alternatives

The coach will assist you to find the best alternatives for your job, career and future goals. They can also assist you to explore alternative courses of action. You are in your own box. Your thoughts, your life experiences and values are all contained within the box. You require an external person to ask you questions to challenge you and stretch you. You cannot get out of your box without the assistance of a coach to stretch you and challenge you. They will suggest alternatives that you never considered because you have been stuck in your own way of thinking. This is very powerful and after this session, you will come away with new ideas and areas where you can grow and learn. Remember, these ideas were already in your mind; however, it will require the coach to ask the right questions to unlock that potential in you.

Provide Feedback

The coach will provide you unbiased feedback on your progress, your habits and behavior. They can provide input where they believe you can improve to gain the desired end state in your life and/or career. This will ensure to keep you on the right track not only in your short-term success but also ensure you are driving towards your life-long goals and objectives.

Preparing for a Coaching Session.

In order to gain the maximum advantage from a coach it is important that you prepare for the session. Take a notepad and pen to take notes. You may also wish to record the session; however, you need to seek the permission of the coach first. Consider what you want to achieve from the coaching session. How will you know if you have achieved this? How can you measure if it was successful or not? Consider the questions you want to ask of your coach to reach your objective. Consider your current reality. Are you happy with your job and career? What challenges do you currently have? Are they technical challenges, lacking experience, leading or managing people? Are you happy in your personal life? Why do you want coaching or advice? Is it personal, career, or your work life balance? If you have lifelong goals or objectives then take these with you for the first session however if you do not have these it does not matter because the coach will ask questions to glean some of these answers from you.

When you meet your coach on subsequent occasions, it is good to answer the following questions and give this feedback to your coach.

This is what I asked._____

This is what you said._____

This is what I learned and applied. _____

Answering these questions and giving this feedback to your coach will let them know that you are serious about your coaching relationship and are applying what you have learned. Myles Downey expresses it this way.

"Coaches are not retained by organizations and line-managers are not expected to coach their direct reports, for fun. The coaching is expected to produce results – measurable returns." [44]

The coach is giving up their valuable time to meet with you. If they take the relationship seriously then they will spend time to prepare for the session, research materials, locate resources and consider their questions. You must ensure that you complete your tasks also. As Keith Ferrazzi writes,

"He cared about me. That is the key to a successful mentorship. A successful mentoring relationship needs equal parts utility and emotion. You cannot simply ask somebody to be personally invested in you. There has to be some reciprocity involved." [41]

Finding a Coach

Keith Ferrazzi, continues, "Mentors are all around you. It's not necessarily your boss or even someone in your business. Mentoring is a non-hierarchical activity that transcends careers and can cross all organizational levels." [41]

You can find a coach through your careers guidance counselor, recruitment agency, or if you are in employment ask your HR representative and they will be happy to help you. For enlightened companies that develop their staff there may be a company intranet that will put you in touch with mentors that are committed to helping you. These mentors come from many areas of the business and all levels of the organization. Access the intranet website and select a mentor based on the skills they have and the areas they wish to coach. These internal coaches are perfect because they already understand the company, the culture and can usually fast track you to the correct people and resources within the organization. This should be your first step if you are looking for a coach. Remember coaches can assist you to go further than you would if you were just working on your own.

You can also find coaches in the city or country where you live. Access the International Coach Federation website for an individual coach where you live. (See website www.x4gy.com)

If you require leadership coaching then a good source would be John Maxwell Coaching. There are coaches in most states and countries. (See website www.x4gy.com)

For quick access to www.x4gy.com scan this QR code

X Factors

- Identify if there are key skills you are lacking.
- Establish what do you want to achieve from a coach
- Search for a coach within your organization, social or voluntary group or seek a professional
- Be committed to the process and do not waste their time.
- A coach will take you further and quicker in your personal and career development than you can go yourself.

Chapter 10

Developing Your Financial Intelligence (FQ)

"If you have not acquired more than a bare existence in the years since we were youth, it is because you either have failed to learn the laws that govern the building of wealth, or else you do not observe them."

– George S. Clason

Introduction

From the outset of this chapter I would like to say that I am not a Financial Advisor. I am not involved in the financial industry in any way. I am not qualified to provide financial advice. The observations I discuss in this chapter are an example of how I manage my personal finances and my long-term wealth creation strategy. If you find any of my comments, observations or strategies interesting then seek advice from a qualified Financial Advisor.

Personal finance is 80% behavior and 20% knowledge. In this chapter I will provide you with some of the 20% that will increase your Financial Intelligence (FQ). I will also outline the behaviors you require, however, you need to work on these yourself.

The old Industrial Age thinking was to work hard at school, go to university, get a good degree, join a large corporation or blue chip company, work there until you retire and then leave with a good pension and benefits package. The old Industrial Age thinking is long gone. Firstly it is very difficult for graduates to get good jobs. Many start in low-paying jobs, while some have large student loans to pay off. When they manage to secure a job, this job is not guaranteed for life. No job is guaranteed anymore. The chance of working for a large company, any company, for 40 years or your whole career, is very unlikely.

The working population is more mobile and transient. For Generation Y the average person may have multiple jobs in their working lifetime. The old Industrial Age thinking said that the more senior you were in the organization and the more years of service meant better salary and perks. When you reached retirement age then the company would provide a good pension and you could retire with a good standard of living. Some companies also offered early retirement and this was an added bonus and some employees with long service, after meeting certain conditions, could retire in their late 50's or early 60's.

For Generation Y these lucrative pension provisions by large corporates are all but dead. The modern era we live in will require you to work until you reach the government / state retirement age. If you have not built your own retirement nest egg with astute retirement planning and investments then you will retire in poverty. If you are unfortunate, you may not even reach retirement age. Those with high salaries will be on the radar for cost cutting, downsizing or outsourcing your role to a lower cost based country. Do not rely on the government or your company to build your retirement fund. You do not want a government or company determining when you can retire. It is your responsibility and it is never too early to start.

Robert T. Kiyosaki, in his book, *Increase your Financial IQ*, writes,

"If you do not believe the rules of money have changed, you're toast. If you think it is smart to work hard, save your money and invest in a well-diversified portfolio of mutual funds, you will become poor." [45]

In this brief chapter on Financial Intelligence, I will explain some cornerstones you should put in place to build your long-term provision for retirement. I know what you are thinking, 'I am Generation Y and it's too early to be thinking of retirement planning.' The 2 best times to plant a tree are today and 30 years ago. Your retirement planning is similar so start today.

Build your Power Team

During your career you will need to build a good and reliable group of advisors that you can trust to give you good independent advice. A financial advisor is one of the first people you will need. They can advise you on products to protect your income and long-term savings products. Choosing a financial advisor can be very difficult. The financial legislation is getting more and more complex and this is driving out the poor financial advisors from the industry. Check that the professionals who are left are going to be in the industry for the long-term. You require an advisor that is with you for the long-term and not someone new to the industry that just wants to sell you the latest financial product to make him/her a big commission.

A good bank manager is also very useful if you require raising capital for an investment opportunity. Many banks today do not offer personal bankers, however, it is important to build a good relationship with a local bank and meet the advisors regularly. They are a good source of information and guidance as you try and grow your nest egg.

A tax accountant is invaluable. Your biggest monthly outgoing is tax. Therefore this should be minimized as much as possible. It is important to pay tax in order to live in safety and security in a modern and well-equipped city and country, however, do not pay more than you need to. Your tax accountant will advise what investment strategies are suitable for recovery of tax. This is your biggest expense and effort should be made to reduce your tax liability.

In addition to a formal team of professional advisors your spouse or partner are critical to your long-term wealth creation strategy. There is little point having a good professional team and good *Offensive Team*, the main breadwinner earning a good salary, if the *Defensive Team*, the partner that does not work and stays at home, spends all the money and more! A good financial partnership is where the Offensive and Defensive team work in unison to build long-term wealth. Ensure that you and your partner have the same behavior when it comes to money. You should both be frugal and careful with every cent or penny. If you are miss-aligned with your partner then more money will go out of the back door than in the front door.

First Things First - Protecting Your Income

After you have built your key financial team, it is now time to protect your income. In most cases this is your salary from your primary job.

It is important to protect your income and revenue stream. Dave Ramsay in his book, *Complete Guide to Money*, writes,

"Your income is your most powerful wealth-building tool." [13]

You can lose your income in 3 ways. You fall ill, you retire or you die. You should protect these 3 ways of losing your income in order to protect your family and you long-term opportunity to build wealth. I know this is not an exciting subject but unfortunately, the only things we can guarantee in life are death and taxes. Sickness and retirement come a close second. For tax advice speak to a professional tax accountant, for the other points then we will address below.

- **You Fall ill** – If you become sick or if you unfortunately have a long-term medical disability that will not allow you to work, then a good company may provide short to medium-term financial support; however, it is your responsibility to make a provision for your long-term financial needs. Consider talking to your financial advisor about Disability Insurance in the event that you have a long-term medical problem or terminal illness.

- **You Retire** – At some point in your life you will retire, however, for our governments to balance their pension arrangements it would be better if we worked until we died! If you plan to retire and have a reasonable standard of living in retirement to the level you enjoy during your working life then you need to start providing for your long-term retirement. Start this saving provision immediately. For Generation Y, time is on your side. Time will build up your pension gradually and will ride out any of the stock market crashes or economic slides for the remaining 30 – 45 years that you have remaining to work. Your financial advisor will explain the pension products available to you and those that are tax efficient.

- **You Die** – When you die, for this is a certainty, you need to ensure that your family is well provided for. If you have a dependant partner or young family then it is important to have proper provision in the event that you have an accident or die prematurely. You do not want your family to live in poverty or have your partner trying to search for a job at a heartbreaking time following your death. If you are employed then a good company may provide some form of Life Assurance cover as part of your salary package. Speak to your Human Resources department for the details. Seek advice from a financial advisor about cheap Term Assurance or other Life Assurance products to protect your family. The level of assurance cover should, at the bare minimum, cover your level of debt on your primary home. In addition, a policy that provides a lump sum for your family to live on is also wise.

Pensions are also Ill, Retiring and Dying

Government, public entities and large companies used to promote the DB (Defined Benefit) pensions as an additional perk for employees. The long-term effect of financing these pension products was very high and many companies have now withdrawn these products for new employees and frozen them for existing employees. The DB pension is very ill, retired and almost dead! Government and large companies can no longer afford to fund these types of pensions because the erratic nature of the stock market has ensured that the returns from equities cannot fund the guaranteed benefits that these schemes afforded. The diminishing pension pot could also not support the growing number of pensioners and reducing workforce.

Now DC (Defined Contribution) pensions are the norm. You put in a defined level of your salary and your company may contribute a percentage. The percentage and contribution are different from company to company and the tax advantages are different by country so you should seek professional advice. It is worth trying to maximize the tax advantages of these schemes and contribute to your pension before tax. This is another way to reduce your tax which is your biggest monthly expenditure.

Your retirement package will be less lucrative and with new government legislation you will need to work longer to secure a state benefit pension. Don't rely on the government to secure your financial future when you retire. Governments are not known for being able to manage money very well and your future is at risk if you rely on them

100% for your long term financial future. You can use the state and company pensions schemes to support your own personal pension arrangements but do not rely on them for your primary income or you will retire poor. Don't plan to retire poor. Your expenses during retirement should be much less therefore calculate what you need to live on when the children have left home and the mortgage on your primary property is paid off.

You will never save yourself to retirement. Inflation and taxes will eat away at your nest egg very quickly and you can never build up a large enough pot of cash to live for 20-30 years after you retire. E.g. If we keep the numbers simple and assume that you start work at the age of 20 and work until you are 60. You have 40 years to save for retirement. Let's also assume you live until you are 80. You then need to finance your retirement for 20 years after you retire. In this simple example you would need to save one third of your net salary during your working life! Some of us struggle to save 10% of our salary therefore one third will be very difficult. If you live beyond 80 years then the problem is more acute.

You need to leverage your cash and invest in revenue producing assets. This will be discussed more fully in subsequent blogs so check the website. In the short remaining time we have together let me describe the main cornerstone of a good financial foundation, your monthly budget.

Stanley and Danko write,

"Wealth is more often the result of a lifestyle of hard work, perseverance, planning and, most of all, self-discipline." [46]

Budgeting

Treat your job like a business. You are the CEO of your own company; (Me Inc, Me Ltd or Me SA).

You have a turnover each month, this is your salary. You have operating costs each month these are your personal expenses. What remains at the end of the month is your profit. A company that does not make a profit every month or year will not be in business for very long. A company that does not have reserves to take it through the lean times will also not be in business for the long-term. You are no different. A company makes profit by maximizing their turnover and minimizing the operating costs. You in turn must maximize your salary and minimize your monthly expenses.

If you spend all your money and a little extra, every month then you are never going to build long-term wealth for retirement. Do you find that you have too much <u>month</u> left at the end of your <u>money</u>? Then you need to review your monthly budget. You cannot afford to leave your current job and if you are downsized or your job is out-sourced then you are in serious trouble. Review your spending and how you service your debt and align your finances to make a profit every month and build your long-term reserves.

Make a decision to live within your means and save a minimum of 10% every month. Thomas Stanley and William Danko describe the definition of being wealthy in their book, *The Millionaire Next Door*. Take your annual Gross Salary and divide by 10. Multiply this number by your age. This figure is your Net Worth. [46] If your Net worth is higher than this figure then you are wealthy. If it is lower then you have some work to do to align your finances and build long-term wealth.

(Gross Salary / 10) x Age = Net Worth

At the beginning of each month plan where each \$, £ or € will go. As Ramsay says in his book, "Give every dollar a name." [13] Do not wait until the end of the month and wonder where all the money has gone. Plan at the start of the month and decide the money you will allocate to charity, rent, mortgage, living expenses, food, clothing, car, insurance and savings. The remainder goes to reserves for an emergency fund and retirement. You need to actively budget for a surplus. Do not wait until the end of the month and wonder where all your money has gone. This is a very poor way to manage your finances.

Plan every expense and the amount for each expense at the beginning of the month. Plan to save at least 10% and place it into a reserve account. This reserve account invested wisely will ensure you match *The Millionaire Next Door* formula and build long-term wealth.

Stanley and Danko sum up this sentiment by saying that,

"Most people have it all wrong about wealth in America. Wealth is not the same as income. If you make a good income each year and spend it all, you are not getting wealthier. You are just living high. Wealth is what you accumulate, not what you spend." [46]

You need to be able to manage your emotions, hopefully you have already read chapter 8. If you can manage your emotions and delay gratification then you have a much better chance of managing your money. Do not go out and spend money if you are having a bad day at the office or you are upset. This is also a poor way to manage your spending. Be controlled and plan your spending at the beginning of each month and maintain this plan throughout the month.

Parkinson's Law, written by author, Parkinson Cyril Northcote, defines a clear law why most people do not accumulate wealth. He defines how your living expense rise with your income and you spend all of your income plus a little more. Do not get into this trap. If you salary rises then live on your original level of expenses, save and invest the remainder to build wealth. Have you thought about when you were a student or during the first job you ever had? You lived a Spartan existence and kept costs low, you survived and times were reasonably good. You then took a job, moved jobs, or had a promotion and in turn you salary increased. You may have found that you moved to a bigger house, bought a better car and spent more money on living expenses. You still spent all you had and although your salary may be considerably higher, you are not accumulating wealth for retirement. You are not working for yourself anymore. You are now in the rat race working for your company. You are on a constant wheel of earning every month, spending all you earn and a little more! George S. Clason, in his book, *The Richest Man in Babylon*, puts it like this,

"That what each of us calls our necessary expenses will always grow to equal our income unless we protest to the contrary." [47]

These wise words, although written in 1926, are still valid for Generation Y today. If you can align your monthly expenses to be less than your monthly income then this is a critical X-Factor in your wealth creation.

Budget Example

At the start of each month, or just after you have been paid by your employer calculate your budget. If your net salary (after tax) is **$2000** or £2000 per month then an example budget could look like this.

Category	Guideline %	Amount
Charity	10 – 15%	200
Rent / Mortgage	No more than 30%	600
Living Expenses	10%	200
Food	20%	400
Utilities - Gas / Electric	5%	100
Car	10%	200
Insurance	5%	100
Savings / Emergency Fund	10%	200
Total		2000

For more assistance on budgeting refer to the excellent materials that Dave Ramsay has to offer in his book, *Complete Guide to Money.* [13]

Investing Primer

Decide which asset class will be the best long-term investment vehicle for you. Forget cash as interest rates are low and the inflation rate in some countries is higher than the interest rate. To calculate your real return, take the interest rate from the savings after tax and then subtract the inflation rate. This will provide you with the actual interest rate you are receiving from your savings. The government taxes any interest you receive from your savings; they then pump billions of dollars, sterling or euros into the economy, which in turn produces inflation. This is the *hidden* tax on your money. Kiyosaki writes,

"Most people don't realize that the rules of money have changed and that if they are savers, they are losers." [45]

X4GY.com Pyramid of Investing [TM]

Retain the minimum of cash required for any household emergencies and then invest the remainder in the asset class of your choice. You could invest in commodities such as gold or silver, equities such as the stock market or property. We began the book with Abraham Maslow's Pyramid of Needs and we end the book with the X4GY Pyramid of Investing™. The explanation about the investments principals can be found on the website.

In the meantime you should consider investing at the bottom of the pyramid; everyone needs food, water, energy, somewhere to live and medication for survival. These physiological needs will never disappear and are solid areas to invest over the long-term.

X Factors

- Build your Power Team
- Protect your Income
- Start your long term pension planning
- Prepare your budget each month and plan for a surplus
- Consider which long-term wealth creation vehicle you will use

I have provided some basic advice to develop your financial intelligence (FQ) and build the foundation for long-term wealth creation. If you are interested in more information about developing long-term wealth then please check the website.

www.x4gy.com

I wish you every success in your personal & career development.

Stuart

Bibliography

[1] M. &. C. D. P. Buckingham, Now Discover Your Strengths, New York, NY: The Free Press, 2001.

[2] K. Green, "Mindset for Success," *Studying the Attitudes and Personalities of High Achievers,* p. 6, 2011.

[3] N. Hill, Think and Grow Rich, Chichester, UK: Capstone Publishing Ltd, 1937.

[4] C. D. Abrashoff, It's Your Ship, New York, New York: Business Plus, Grand Central Publishing, 2002.

[5] R. Aaron, Branding Small Business for Dummies, Ontario, Canada: John Wiley & Sons, 2013.

[6] D. Patten, How to Market Your Business, London: Kogan Page, 2008.

[7] D. Evans, Social Media Marketing, Indianapolis: Wiley Publishing Inc, 2008.

[8] L. Brown, "National Achievers Congress,19th and 20th October," Amsterdam, Netherlands, 2013.

[9] C. K. Goman, "www.forbes.com," 2nd February 2011. [Online]. Available: http://www.forbes.com/sites/carolkinseygoman/2011/02/13/seven-seconds-to-make-a-first-impression/. [Accessed 25th October 2013].

[10] D. D. Lewis, The Secret Language of Success, London, UK: Bantam Press, 1989.

[11] N. Hill, Outwitting the Devil, New York, NY: Sterling Publishing Co.Inc., 1938.

[12] J. Olson, The Slight Edge, Lake Dallas, Texas: R & L Publishing Ltd, 2011.

[13] D. Ramsay, Complete Guide to Money, Brentwood, TN: Lampo Press, The Lampo Group Inc., 2011.

[14] J. Maxwell, Sometimes You Win Sometimes You Learn, New York, NY: Center Street, 2013.

[15] T. Eker, Secrets of the Millionaire Mind, New York, NY: Piatkus Books, 2005.

[16] J. Maxwell, 21 Laws of Leadership, Nashville, TN: Thomas Nelson Inc., 2007.

[17]   T. Robbins, "FaceBook Post," FaceBook Post, 26th October 2013. [Online]. Available: https://www.facebook.com/#!/TonyRobbins/posts/10151860837184060. [Accessed 26th October 2013].

[18]   L. S. Coe, "National Achievers Congress 2012," in *Success Resources*, London, UK, 2012.

[19]   A. Mandossian, "American Communications Network," in *Annual Conference*, Budapest, 2013.

[20]   R. Templar, The Rules of Management, Harlow, UK: Pearson Prentice Hall Business, 2005.

[21]   M. H. McCormack, What They Still Don't Teach You At Harvard Business School, New York, NY: Bantam Books, 1989.

[22]   H. B. Publishing, "www.harvardbusiness.org," [Online]. Available: http://www.harvardbusiness.org/harvard-managementor. [Accessed 5th November 2013].

[23]   P. Hoang, Business and Management, Victoria, Australia: IBID Press, 2007.

[24]   P. Leish, Effective Leadership, London, UK: Straightforward Publishing Ltd, 1997.

[25]   B. a. Mouton, "Blake and Mouton Leadership Grid," 2013. [Online]. Available: http://www.makeadentleadership.com/blake-and-mouton.html. [Accessed 4th October 2013].

[26]   J. P. Kotter, "http://www.kotterinternational.com/our-principles/changesteps," 2012. [Online]. Available: http://www.kotterinternational.com/our-principles/changesteps. [Accessed 29th October 2013].

[27]   M. Rouse, "www.whatis.techtarget.com/contributor/Margaret-Rouse," September 2010. [Online]. Available: http://searchcio-midmarket.techtarget.com/definition/change-management. [Accessed 29th October 2013].

[28]   J. Maxwell, The 21 Irrefutable Laws of Leadership, 10th Anniversary Edition, Nashville, Tennesse: Thomas Nelson Inc, 2007.

[29]   J. Kennedy, "http://history1900s.about.com/od/1960s/a/jfkmoon_3.htm," http://history1900s.about.com/od/1960s/a/jfkmoon_3.htm, [Online]. Available: http://history1900s.about.com/od/1960s/a/jfkmoon_3.htm. [Accessed 6th November 2013].

[30] M. S. Goodyear, "www.goodyear.com," Goodyear Tires, 2010-2013. [Online]. Available: http://www.goodyear.com/mission/global_purpose.html. [Accessed 6th November 2013].

[31] J. P. Kotter, Leading Change, Boston, MA: Harvard Business School Press, 1996.

[32] T. &. G. J. Bradberry, Emotional Intelligence 2.0, San Diego, CA: Talentsmart, 2009.

[33] D. J. Goleman, "BrainyQuote.com," BrainyQuote.com, 2001-2013. [Online]. Available: http://www.brainyquote.com/quotes/authors/d/daniel_goleman.html. [Accessed 30th October 2013].

[34] J. West, "www.sff.net," www.sff.net, 21 March 2002. [Online]. Available: http://www.sff.net/people/julia.west/callihoo/dtbb/feelings.htm. [Accessed 1st November 2013].

[35] M. O'Conner, "www.dailymail.co.uk," You've got 7 seconds to impress me, 13th December 2010. [Online]. Available: http://www.dailymail.co.uk/femail/article-1338064/Youve-got-7-seconds-impress-How-size-men-time.html. [Accessed 1st November 2013].

[36] A. Mehrabian, "Businessballs.com," Business Balls, 2004-2012. [Online]. Available: http://www.businessballs.com/mehrabiancommunications.htm. [Accessed 1st November 2013].

[37] C. K. Goman, "www.forbes.com," 2md February 2011. [Online]. Available: http://www.forbes.com/sites/carolkinseygoman/2011/02/13/seven-seconds-to-make-a-first-impression/. [Accessed 25th October 2013].

[38] A. &. P. B. Pease, The Definitive Book or Body Language, London: Pease International Pty Ltd, 2005.

[39] G. Zalucki, "American Network Communications," in *Annual Conference*, Budapest, 2013.

[40] J. Whitmore, Coaching for Performance, London, UK: Nicholas Brealey Publishing, 2013.

[41] K. Ferrazzi, Never Eat Alone, New York, NY: Doubleday, Random House Inc., 2005.

[42] I. C. Federation, "International Coaching Federation," International Coaching Federation, 2012. [Online]. Available: http://foundation.coachfederation.org/AboutCoaching.aspx. [Accessed 2nd November 2013].

[43] T. Stoltzfus, Coaching Questions - A Coach's Guide to Powerful Asking Skills, Virginia Beach, VA: www.coach22.com, 2008.

[44] M. Downey, Effective Coaching - Lessons from the Coach's Coach, London, UK: Cengage Learning, 2003.

[45] T. R. Kiyosaki, Increase Your Financial IQ, New York, NY: Hachette Book Group Inc., 2008.

[46] T. J. &. D. W. D. Stanley, The Millionaire Next Door, New York, NY: Pocket Books, Longstreet Press Inc, 1996.

[47] G. S. Clason, The Richest Man in Babylon, New York, NY: New American Library, Penguin Group (USA) Inc., 1926.

[48] "Strengths Finders," [Online]. Available: https://www.gallupstrengthscenter.com/.

Personal Notes

CPSIA information can be obtained at www.ICGtesting.com
Printed in the USA
BVOW02s1412261213

340135BV00007B/120/P